Fabio Ribeiro de Araujo (c)
2nd Edition

SELECTED PROPHECIES AND PROPHETS

With their authenticity critiqued

Fabio Ribeiro de Araujo
2nd Edition

SELECTED PROPHECIES AND PROPHETS

With their authenticity critiqued

Liber Mirabilis, Legenda Aurea, Signa Judicii, Alois
Irlmaier, Gioacchino di Fiore, Pseudo-Methodius, Monk
Adso, Brigita of Sweden, Mother Shipton, St. Malachy, St.
Hildegard, Savonarola, Nostradamus, Orval Prophecy etc.

Araujo, Fabio R.

Selected Prophecies and Prophets. With their authenticity critiqued - Fabio R. Araujo– 2nd ed.

   1. History 2. Prophecies

ook carefully at the original painting above by the Italian painter Gianluca de Grossi. This book cover is the image you see above with a few changes (darkened to reflect the prophecies on the three days of darkness.) The painting is a dream this Italian painter had years ago, in the 1990s. The following day, he was very surprised when he learned that one of his sisters had had exactly the same dream. At that night, both "saw" themselves watching their Italian city underwater from the same room on the last floor of their family house over the hills of Bologna. There was also a common feeling "I knew it would happen". Years later, when he told me his dream in an Italian restaurant, around 2005, I asked him to paint what he saw. He didn't know there are many prophecies about a future global flood, because he had never read anything about it. I don't believe this could be just a coincidence, the probability of brother and sister having exactly the same dream at the same night is very small. What about you?

Please visit his website at www.degrossi.it for more nice surrealist paintings.

TABLE OF CONTENTS

PREFACE

enturies ago, some religious people, priests, bishops etc. spent a large part of their lives trying to understand what the old prophets and books could reveal about the future of mankind. Based on a biblical and theological viewpoint, they tried to find out what could have been predicted in and out of the Bible. Typical topics found were the end of the world, the Antichrist, the second coming of Christ, the Great Monarch, a final reformation in the Church, a Holy Pope, and a final religious war against the forces enemies of Christ. Some of those men and women called prophets announced some real predictions, through a vision, voices heard, dreams etc. while others just studied the matter for years and had their conclusions.

While some of these prophets or researchers of prophecy were considered wise people, some of these discoverers of the future were even burned, such as Savonarola in Ferrara and Giordano Bruno in Rome, both in Italy, where there was a huge control for new prophecies under the Inquisition and any book with a unexpected matter was censored (prohibited parts were covered in red or some pages were removed) or totally destroyed. Some other people went to jail for studying and writing about prophecies, such as Father António Vieira, who was sent from Brazil back to Portugal and spent 22 months in prison for writing a book called *Clavis Prophetarum* and the 14th century priest Jean of Cleft Rock or Rupescissa, who spent part of his life in prison in the Palace of the Popes in Avignon, France. Many others misinterpreted prophecies in heretical movements and believed the reformation of the Church and the end of times were both close, including Luther, who thought the Antichrist was living during his time and was the Pope himself. Some had a better life and were famous even while alive. Nostradamus, for example, had his presence demanded by

Queen Cathérine in her palace to foresee the future of France. And, as some people claim, Hitler had his private astrologers.

Understanding a prophecy is not an easy task. If in the past, it led people to the fire and to prison, today, it continues to be a hard job to interpret prophecies and to criticize their authenticity. Most of the books in the market only list the prophecy without even trying to evaluate seriously its authenticity and sometimes the hermeneutics or interpretation is poor due of the writer's lack of knowledge in the matter.

After about 20 years reading them, I believe the best method to analyze a prophecy is the same used by Historians and this is well explained in the manual of history written by Charles-Victor Langlois and Charles Seignobos in France and published in 1898, based on Ranke ideas born in Germany a few years before. If the link is still valid, the table of contents of this book is reproduced in the following link: http://www.umass.edu/wsp/methodology/outline/langlois.html

Basically, the analytical operations are divided in external criticism and internal criticism. External criticism means checking the authorship or authenticity of the text or prophecy, in this case. We need to know, first of all, if the prophet really wrote that prophecy. Many manuscripts are not authentic and people keep forging prophecies today through Internet.

The second step is called internal criticism. Basically it means to get knowledge to understand properly what a prophet wrote hundreds or thousands of years ago. If a prophet saw "flying metallic grasshoppers" it might refer to war planes and this way the authentic prophecy written by Leonardo da Vinci below, which I translated from old Italian, is easier to understand:

Many men will be seen in animals moving very quickly towards the end of their lives and in a very quick death. Through the air and over the land

animals will be seen in many colors carrying ferociously the men to the destruction of their lives.

It also means that when Nostradamus predicted for 1999 "the King of Angolmois lives again", we need to open the books of history to find out, first of all, where was Angoulmois. Once we find it out, we might ask: Were there any Dukes there? When? Angoulmois was a medieval province of France. Yes, there were Dukes there in the Middle Ages and a little later. The "King of Angoulmois" mentioned by Nostradamus is probably the King of France Francis I, who was Duke in Angoulmois. Why Francis I and not another Duke? Because Francis I was the King of France when Nostradamus was alive. Probably Francis I is not going to live again, but a powerful European political leader will fight the United Europe, as Francis I did in the 16th century, having Muslims as allies. Putin came to power as President of Russia in the last day of 1999. He is probably the King of Angoumois Nostradamus predicted. This is internal criticism.

These 2 criticisms add seriousness to the work of writing about prophecies and interpreting them. Prophecy and premonition happen all the time. There are many books about that. People have dreams about facts all the time that are fulfilled. The website *www.prophecies.us* has an example of how the plane crash in the Hudson river, New York in January 2009, was predicted.

Years ago a similar thing happened to another person. It was 1998, December if I remember well. This person from Yugoslavia wrote a message in a group of people interested in prophecies that he was having dreams about a city destroyed in a war. Nobody seemed to care about what he posted. He was seeing numbers related to the dream too. There was a week, a month and a year related to the war event. A few months later, in the same week, month, and year, a war break out in Yugoslavia in 1999. In February 2003, Yugoslavia was renamed to State Union of Serbia and Montenegro and in 2006, both Montenegro and Serbia declared indepence, ending the Yugoslavia state.

This means my interpretation was wrong in the beginning but the prophecy was real. This happens in almost any book when the writer tries to understand the prophecy. Naturally, people create prophecies all the time and we cannot believe in anything we read on the net, but these two previous examples show clearly we have a skill we still do not understand very well.

I am unable to explain how is it possible to know the future or why not everyone has dreams or visions about it. But when someone asks how is it possible to know the future I ask myself "do we know what time is?" I have my opinion about it but I don't think it is the right place to expose it. This book is basically a compilation of prophecies not an explanatory work about premonition or prophecy.

I tried to do the best I could in this work. I checked the source when possible. It took me years to research the prophets mentioned, and it included visits to European libraries, manuscripts in Latin checked and hundreds of books read in many languages. I also met and exchanged e-mail with some of the best European and American prophecy experts, some known worldwide, some of tem being the best in the world in their field of expertise.

This book contains texts translated from Latin, German, French, Italian, Spanish and Portuguese. It seems that at least one prophecy was never published in English before. This book is fruit of a research that began about 20 years ago after a kind of vision I had (the only one so far), which changed my life and lead me to research and understand prophecies. This is why I wrote this book. Hopefully you will find it reasonably useful.

Fabio R. Araujo, Historian
www.prophezeiung.net

And thus a Min said to R. Abbahu: 'When will the Messiah come?' He replied, 'When darkness covers those people.' 'You curse me, he exclaimed. He retorted, 'it is but a verse: *For, behold, the darkness shall cover the earth, and gross darkness the people: but the Lord shall shine upon thee, and his glory shall be seen upon thee.*'

Tractate Sanhedrin[1] – Folio 99 A

---

[1] Old Jewish book, attributed to Moses, first referenced at 57 BC.

INTRODUCTION

"When you see the abomination of the devastation in the holy land... those who are in the fields, flee to the mountains, and those who are on the roof, do not come down to take what you have at home". Mt. 24, 15-17 and Mc. 13, 14-15

"And if God hadn't shortened these days, nobody would survive". Mt. 24, 20 and Mc. 13, 22

*F*or centuries, the most respectful religious people and writers have interpreted the prophecy above concerning the abomination of the desolation or devastation as the Antichrist. The "abomination of the devastation in the holy land" was interpreted as the Antichrist on the throne in the Temple of Jerusalem after rebuilding it. Passages like these blew and inspired the imagination of many people, allowing the composition of wonderful and detailed manuscripts throughout the times, such as the one written by Monk Adso, called *Libellus de Antechristo,* or maybe the Visions of Hildegard, and the initial part of the Legenda Aurea, the first best-selling publication in Europe in the years 1470-1530, when the New World was being conquered.

Who would be this Antichrist, predicted to come in the end of the world? He would be a very powerful political leader who, at the end of times, would rule over mankind and kill all people who believed in Christ. The evil ones would prevail and only they would survive. Or maybe Christ would come back before this final battle and save the good people killing the Antichrist.

If you read those two biblical passages on the top of the last page, you probably will not understand how a person can escape from the Antichrist only for being on the roof of his house. If this prophecy is really about the Antichrist, will he be blind? Maybe he will not know this prophecy about himself and won't look for Christians who hide themselves on the roof of their houses, if they can't find a better place to hide. Or maybe this wicked miracle-maker will not have access to a helicopter. Couldn't this prophecy be predicting a huge flood possibly caused by the melting of the polar ices in our planet, linked someway to the global warming that we feel today, as it is predicted in many different cultures and sources of all ages? A huge tsunami? If so, it makes sense, and those who are in the fields will need to flee to the mountains to survive, and those in the cities need to be on the roofs to survive, forgetting their belongings inside their houses, praying to everything go back to normal to save their lives as quick as possible. In fact, the prophecy continues announcing that if these days were longer, people wouldn't survive.

The three largest religions of the world, Hinduism, Islamism and Christianity, have prophecies about a flood. While people in the first years of the global warming talks did not believe in the possibility of a flood, today (2009) scientists admit this possibility and calculations are made to see the impact a flood will cause. Even Google created an engine to show an image with a flooded map if you provide the number of feet or meters for the flood you want to see. Moreover, there are prophecies about people in panic because of the sea, but many scholars still believe that this is just a set of forgeries or creations of an imaginative mind.

The famous French historian Jacques Le Goff explains in one of his books[2] that *"According the Apocalypse attributed to John the disciple, revelation of events near the end of the world, a period initially agitated and*

---

[2] *L'Occident medieval et le temps, Rire au Moyen Age, Le rire dans les règles monastiques du haut Moyen Age.* Éditions Gallimard, 1999

then, on the contrary, calm and happy, will precede the end of the world. A diabolical person, the Antichrist, will reign over the Earth among calamities and wars, but then, after the Antichrist's death, a long period of peace, justice and happiness, the Millennium, will be established. In this time before the end of the world, there will be a special time, 'the last times' or eschatological times. Because the idea of a Millennium on the Earth faced the image of a political, moral and religious upsetting, the Church fought vigorously such belief. However, it had many followers during the Middle Ages and it is found in many heretical movements".

Many prophecies were written in the past centuries from virtually any area in the world. Most of the main historians believe that the prophecies were usually or always created or forged to manipulate people, politically, socially or religiously. Certainly some of them were, and maybe most of them. Even though I'm a historian, I don't think that all of them were. I had what I call a "vision" myself (a premonition) which was fulfilled, and I think that some of these prophecies might be true prophecies, even if used many times in the past in the wrong moments.

The prophecies tend to predict some common issues. They are usually about one or more of the following elements:

o Natural catastrophes, which are the signs of the end of the world, including: Huge waves, a tsunami or a flood, a dark sky (prophecies about the 3 days of darkness), fall of stars etc. Prophecies from virtually any part of the world and many civilizations announce this future catastrophe. These prophecies are older than Christ. The Signa Judicii was one of the most known manuscripts about the signs of the end of the world written in the Middle Ages and it mentioned these natural catastrophes.

o A big world war, a final war, sometimes referred as a religious war, which might be the third world war. The prophecies usually mention the destruction of the main European cities. It's a final war, when the sons of the light or the good ones will battle the sons of darkness or the wicked ones. Many religions spread prophecies about this final moment and the victory of the light over the darkness. These are very old prophecies, older than Christianity.

o The Great Monarch, called King Messiah by the Jews. Some experts such as Jacques Le Goff think that this "myth" was born in the Middle Ages. Mr. Bernard McGinn believes that these myths are rooted in the Ancient Near East and in the biblical traditions, which I totally agree. Other writers also found out that the Messiah belief come from other civilizations[3]. I think it arrived in Europe from the Jews and this is older than Christ, and is already predicted in many Jewish texts, including in the Old Testament, but is prophecies about a future great king is also found in Assyrian tablets. The Jews called this future warrior as King Messiah and this is why they did not accept Christ as their Messiah. It seems that the Jewish prophecies are contradictory and I would risk that there are clearly 2 Messiahs mentioned in their prophecies.[4] I believe that monarchy will come back for some time. It will come back during the third world war and will disappear again about 20 or 30 years later when a new system will be implemented in Germany and will be spread throughout the world. The last country to abandon capitalism and be converted to this future system will be China.

o The Angelical Pope, a Pope who will implement a reformation in the Church. Same thing apply. The world's experts consider this to be a Middle Ages myth, but this is older than Christ. I'm

[3] Wallis, Wilson. Messiahs: *Christian and Pagan*. Richard G Badger, 1918 and *Messiahs, Their Role in Civilization*. American Council on Public Affairs, 1943
[4] The book *The Second Messiah* written by Christopher Knight and Robert Lomas links the Second Messiah to a secret kept by the Freemasonry and the Templars. There is also a Catar legend about 2 Sons of God.

sure this comes from the Jews too, because his prophecies can be found in the Old Testament.

o A Reformation in the Church, linked to the Great Monarch and the Angelical Pope and the reestablishment of the Monarchy in many countries. These are typically catholic prophecies and, as Jacques Le Goff says, were used many times in the past linked to the belief of end of world.

o The Antichrist. The personification of the Antichrist seems to be born with Ireneaus, Bishop of Lyon, who lived in the 2nd century, the first to say that the antichrist would be a Jew, which certainly motivated persecutions during the Middle Ages. I think that these are typically catholic prophecies too, and were born with the first followers of Christ. In his book called *Tischreden*, we can see that Luther used the general belief on the Antichrist to state that the current Pope was the Antichrist and then the end of the world was close, so a change was necessary.

o Civil wars in Europe seeming to be related to a religious cause, which break out a few weeks before the big war. Alois Irlmaier says clearly that Paris will be destroyed by its inhabitants, in a civil conflict; the city should be set on fire. I believe this will be conflicts between Muslims and Christians, but all living in Europe.

The Angelical Pope and the Great Monarch are the two most predicted people in the history of our planet. As Simo Parpola [5] showed recently in his researches translating tablets recently-found in Mesopotamia, some Jewish beliefs came from other people, such as the Assyrians. It's known that the Psalm 104 came from the Egyptians, as it is written in a wall in ruins in Egypt. The Jewish beliefs on the King Messiah might have come from the East and might be even older than 2500 years.

---

[5] Parpola, Simo. *Assyrian Prophecies*. Helsinki: Helsinki University Press, 1997

This is an Old Testament prophecy about the Great Monarch on the throne in the Temple and the priest:

"It is he who shall build the temple of the LORD and shall bear royal honor, and shall sit and rule on his throne. And there shall be a priest on his throne, and the counsel of peace shall be between them both" (Zechariah 6:13).

This comes from Mesopotamia, a 3000 year old prophecy:

"The rivers will give fish, the fields will produce rich fruits, the winter food will last until the summer and the summer foods will last until the winter... The evil will become order, the darkness will disappear, and the evil will vanish. Clouds won't lack, the brother will feel compassion for his brother... This monarch will rule over all the peoples... He will destroy Elam (old name for an area where Iran is today), he will destroy its cities." (Nineveh Tablet III 6-24, written 3000 years ago)

Chapter 1.

Father Caliste

*A*ccording to some French books published in the 19th century, such as the famous *Voix Prophétiques*,[6] the prophecy attributed to Father Calixte or Caliste arrived to us through a letter written on December 3rd 1750, sent from a priest, Dom Madrigas, at Cluny Abbey, France, to the prior at the Moutier-Saint-Jean-en-Auxois Abbey, in Bourgogne.

According to this French book author, Abbot Curicque, this prophecy became known thanks to a copy of the original letter, which was sent to him from England. Based on the introduction in the copy, the letter was kept in secret for some time due to religious politics. The copy had the inscription *Au Rév. Père Prieur de l'Abbaye de Montier-Saint-Jean, en Auxois, Bourgogne.*

It seems that the first time this letter was published was in an Italian book called *I Futuri Destini*, in 1871, not in the *Voix Prophétiques*. I checked both versions and the letters printed in the *Voix Prophétiques* and in *I Futuri Destini* are a little different. I translated the version here from the *Voix Prophétiques,* which seemed to me more genuine.

Naturally, the letter could have been forged, as some prophecies definitively were in the past, especially during Middle Ages, when

---

[6] Printed in 1872 in France, this 2 volume work was written by an Abbot, Mr. Curicque, who was also a member in the Archaeology and History Society (Société d'Archéologie et d'Histoire) in Moselle.

manuscript communication was easy to forge, but if this really happened, the fraud was well done, and it is hard to say if the prophecy is authentic today.

The prophetic letter announces some past events that were fulfilled and it also predicts some future events, such as huge waves, a war, the great monarch, the angelical pope and the revival of faith in a period of peace after these two natural and human catastrophes. All these topics (the waters, the war, the great monarch etc.) are among the most predicted in history.

"My Venerable Father,

It's still shaking that I take the pen to give you knowledge of a happening that dismayed our house.

We were in the morning exercise, the holy Mass was finishing. In the deepest silence, a voice arises suddenly. It was the voice of one of our priests, a simple man, but with a great faith:

"Misfortune to us!... Misfortune to us!..."

Saying these words, he turned his face down as if to calm God down, who he was seeing irritated.

The astonishment and the terror took possession of all of us. His figure seemed resplendent to us and his look was shiny. He was speaking in hardness, but clearly and slowly, what allow us to write his revelation down, which we transmit attached, without changing the order in which he predicted these terrible happenings.

Revelation of Father Caliste, December 1st, 1750.

"The vengeance of God is coming, the time urges, penitence, you sinners! The iniquity flooded the land, this is nothing but iniquity. Which saints will pray for us? The celestial vengeance will wait all the sinners. We abused the sacrifice[7], the sacrifice will cease. We are tied to the earth, the land will be taken and we will be taken from the land. The wicked ones' commands will be executed. Death will desolate priests and lays. The heights will be reduced. Three lilies of the royal crown will fall in blood[8], a fourth in the mood[9] and a fifth will be eclipsed[10].

The wicked ones will devour themselves; blood, blood, one will drink. A flaming sword[11] will raise in the sea and, blood red, will plunge back. Twice, the wreckage of a big wreck will be brought through the northern waves. The mercifulness of God will be despised: one will believe to be able to live without his help and He will remove it; He will abandon peoples and kings, the trustees of power will be dispersed. Church of God, thou shalt moan. Ministers of the Lord, you will cry for new profanations. Blood, blood, one will drink, one will drink. The sinner land will be purified through fire and will devour those who sat on the iniquity. A shiny lily[12] gets out of the cloud. Glory to God! Faith is reborn; a man[13], instrument of God, relights the chandelier. Happy will be those who survive! Glory to God!"

Once he stopped speaking, my Venerable Father, he seemed exhausted. A fever seized him and he died yesterday, after thirty hours of illness, during which we couldn't get any additional word. Pray and make others pray for the rest of his soul.

What does all these things mean, my Venerable Father? What are these disgraces that menace us? How similar are the chastisements announced to

---

[7] The Mass
[8] Louis XVI, Marie Antoniete and Isabelle
[9] Marie Terese, Duchess of Angoulême, died in exile after years in prison
[10] The Great Monarch, descending from King Louis XVII, dead or missing
[11] a huge wave, probably
[12] The King
[13] The Angelical Pope

us and those used by God to punish Israel! I transmit you these things so that you let your community know about it and that you inform us the means to pacify God's wrath.

(...)

My advanced age and my astonishment prevent me from having a conclusion. Receive respectfully, my Venerable Father, my best regards.

Don Madrigas
Abbey of Cluny

Chapter 2.

Liber Mirabilis

---

*L*iber Mirabilis or *Mirabilis Liber*[14] was printed for the first time in the beginning of the 16th century. It is not very clear when the first edition of this book was published, but it was probably between 1515 and 1522 in France. According to some reliable information, a second edition was published in 1522 and/or 1523 and another one was published one year later. Many old and new books published in many countries state that its author was Jean of Vatiguerro[15] and that he would have lived in the 13th or in the 16th century. Some writers attribute incorrectly this book to other people, such as Nostradamus father, St. Cesaire, and to a certain Jean Muller, such as Collin Wilson in his book[16].

This book was certainly one of the most important books about prophecy printed in the 16th century in Europe, and some people consider it is the second, following Nostradamus oracles. The book is a comprehensive collection of prophecies and it

---

[14] Mirabilis Liber. Qui Prophetias Revelationesque nec non Res Mirandas Preteritas Presentes et Futuras Aperte Demonstrat.

[15] Those who say he may have lived in the 16th century might not know that Vatiguerro predicted events for the 15th century, so he was an adult in the 15th century. It's not certain that he lived in the 16th century, but he certainly lived in the 15th century. Vatiguerro is not a real name, but a pseudonym, and this person might not have even existed. He is the supposed author of one of the prophecies in the book.

[16] Collin, Wilson. *The Occult.* London: Watkins Publishing, 2003

seems that most of these prophecies were obtained in the Bibliotheque S.Victor or from a book printed in Latin in the end of the 15th century, called *Pronosticatio*. The Liber Mirabilis was "in full vogue" in France in the 1520s and in the 1530s. Expert in Nostradamus Peter Lemesurier believes that this book was the main source of inspiration for Nostradamus' oracles.

During the French Revolution, a curious situation happened in Paris related to this book. It was believed that the Liber Mirabilis contained a prophecy about the French Revolution, and the libraries were forbidden to allow access to this section to the people by the government. Many copies had the second part of this book destroyed and this is the reason why some 16th century copies are still found in libraries in France, such as the St.Genevieve in Paris, without this 2nd section. The government decided the access to the book because suddenly many French people wanted to see this book to check the prophecy.

As one of the volumes of the *Dictionaire des Prophéties et des Miracles*, published in 1855, shows this book is connected to other episodes of history, relating politics and prophecy, in the revolutionary years of 1814, 1830, and 1848, because some people imagined to find in this book the promise of a political restoration fulfilled.

The *Liber Mirabilis* has 2 sections, the first one is in Latin and the second, shorter, is in French. The book has prophecies attributed to Bishop Bemechobus (better known as Pseudo-Methodius), Saint Brigitta or Brigida of Sweden, Sibyl of Crete, Joachim or Gioacchino de Fiore, Jerome Savonarola, Jean de Roche-fendue or Roquetallaide, Jean Precheguerre or Vatiguerro himself, Saint Severe, and many others less known.

I selected the following prophecies from the book, which could not be understood at that time, but can certainly be easily understood today, as they seem to be references to the use of chemical weapons.

"In fact, the land in many areas will shake with fear and it will swallow the living ones: a lot of cities, fortresses and powerful cities will be destroyed by earthquakes. The fruits of the land will decrease and the humidity will disappear; the seeds will rot in the fields and those that will sprout won't give fruits. The sea will emit loud noises and it will raise against the world and it will swallow many ships and many people: The air will be infested and rotten because of the malice of the people's indignity.

Numerous and amazing signs will appear in the sky: the sun will be darkened[17] *and it will have a bloody color for many people. Two moons will appear at once for about four hours: close to them they will see many surprising things worthy of admiration. Many stars will crash themselves with others and this will be the sign for the destruction and slaughter of many men.*

The natural course of the air will be almost completely changed and damaged because of the pestilential illnesses: sudden and several deaths will come for men and animals: there will be an inexplicable plague: a cruel and

---

[17] Three days of darkness

hideous famine will desolate everyone, specially in the West. Never, since the beginning of the world, has one heard of a similar famine".

Another prophecy, which I never saw published in any book, which I found in the *Liber Mirabilis*, predicts the raise of the sea level, also predicted in other sources:

"The oceans will rise over the coasts, that is, over the French coasts, as the mountains (become) similar to plains, and if it were not for an angel, they would be all flooded because of the sin. But this sea will grow through the coasts in a wide and violent way".

Chapter 3.

Monk Adso

*A*uthor of theological treatises and biographies of saints, Monk Adso, Abbot in Mountier-en-Der, also known as Adso de Montier or Adso Dervensis, was born about 910. As Bernard McGinn[18] says, *"he entered the monastic life during the time of the great reforms associated with the houses of Cluny and Gorze"*.

Adso composed a long letter, which is considered a treaty to the Queen Gerberga, wife of the Frank King Louis IV. This letter was written between 949 and 954, and constituted in one of the best and most spread treatises about the Antichrist written in the Middle Ages, called *Epistola Adsonis ad Gergergam Reginam de Ortu et Tempore Antichristi* also known as *Libellus de Antichristo*. It was not by accident that this manuscript quickly became one of the fundamental texts about the eschatological literature in Europe. Emmerson[19] says "that standard exegetical interpretation of Antichrist organized by Adso remained influential in the Middle Ages is evident in two encyclopedic works, the *Compendium theologicae veritatis* (ca. 1265) of Hugh Ripelin of Strassburg (d. 1319) and the *Tractatus de victoria Christi contra Antichristum* (1319) of Hugh of Newcastle (1280-1322)".

---

[18] McGinn, Bernard. Visions of the End. New York: Columbia University Press, 1998
[19] Emmerson, Richard Kenneth. Antichrist in the Middle Ages. Seattle: University of Washington Press, 1981

The hand-written copies, many times without the dedication to the Queen and the reference to the writer, were reproduced many times, sometimes anonymously or attributed to other past writers (Saint Augustine, Rabanus Maurus etc.) with some changes. There is a lot of information about what people thought concerning to the Antichrist in this document, compiled from other older sources.

This work is also important because it says that the end of the world seems to be far, and it reflects what the most important priests at that time (near the millennium) believed: The end of the world was not close because they were coming closer to the year 1000. This fear of the millennium existed among some priests, but the wide repercussion of this fear was a legend created a few centuries later.

In this treaty, Adso mentions many elements that Irenaeus of Lyon wrote in the 2nd century in the text *Adversus Haereses*, as you can see in the next chapter, for example, he believed that the Antichrist would be a Jew, coming from the tribe of Dan:

"Sicut ergo auctores nostri dicunt, Antichristus ex populo Iudeorum nascentur, de tribu scilicet Dan..."

As José Guadalaraja Medina says[20], Adso was a very active man in his time, he participated in a monastic reformation in many French abbeys and was in contact with the most important doctors or scholars at that time. Adso died during a pilgrimage to Jerusalem in 992.

Jacques Le Goff says in his study about Middle Ages[21] that the figure of the antichrist was highlighted in the 8th century by a monk called Peter, who took it from the prophecy attributed to Methodius written in the 7th century and then in the 10th century, in Adso's treaty.

---

[20] Medina. José Guadalaraja. *Las Profecias del Anticristo em Edad Media.* Madrid: Gredos, 1996, page 148
[21] Le Goff, Jacques. *La Civilisation de l'occident medieval.* Paris: Flammarion, 1982

The treaty *De Antechristo*, was sometimes attributed to Saint Augustine, according to a few 19th century experts such as Abbot Lecanu. Different versions or families of the text initially written by Adso can be found in many European libraries, usually with interpolations and adaptations.

Here is a translation from the Latin text *De ortu et tempore Antichristi* ed. E. Sackur, Sibyllinische Texte und Forschungen (1898), 104-113. A few paragraphs were not included in the translation.

"First of all, you want to know why he is called Antichrist. It is because he is against Christ and will act against Christ. Christ was humble, he will be proud. Christ came to raise the humble ones, to reduce the sinners; he will be against humble people and will magnify sinners and exalt the impious ones. He will always praise vices against virtues and will slowly dissipate the Gospel law. He will revive the culture of demons in the world, he will want his own glory and will call himself Almighty God.

The Antichrist has many ministers for malice, many have already existed, like Antiochus, Nero, and Domitian. Even now in our times we know there are many Antichrists. Anyone, be layman, cleric, or monk, who lives against the justice and attacks the rule of his way of life and blasphemes on what is good is an Antichrist, is a minister of Satan.

What I say, I don't create nor say from myself. I found them in books carefully re-read.

Our doctors say that Antichrist will come from the Jewish people, from the tribe of Dan, according to the following prophecy: "Let Dan be a snake in the wayside, an adder on the path".[22] Let he be a snake in the wayside and let he be on the path in order to wound those who walk in the paths of justice[23] and kill them with the poison of his wickedness. He will be born from the

---

[22] Genesis. XLIX-17
[23] Psalm XXII.3

copulation of mother and father, like any man, not, as some say, from a virgin alone. He will be totally conceived in the sin, engendered in the sin, and will come to birth in the sin.

At the beginning of his conception the devil will enter into his mother's womb. The devil's power will foster and protect him in his mother's womb and the evil power will be always with him. As the Holy Spirit came into the mother of Our Lord Jesus Christ and overshadowed her with his power and filled her with divinity, so that she conceived from the Holy Spirit and what came to birth of her was divine and holy, so the devil will descend into the Antichrist's mother, will fill totally her, encompass her, master her, possess her inside and outside, so that with the devil's cooperation she will conceive through a man and what will be born from her will be totally iniquitous, totally evil, totally lost. This is the reason why this man is called the Son of Perdition, because he will destroy humankind as far as he can. You heard how will be his birth. Now, know the place where will be born.

As Our Lord and redeemer chose Bethlehem as the place where he assumed a human body and was born for us, so the same way the devil chose a place for that lost man who is called Antichrist, a place from which the root of all evil shall come, namely Babylon city. This city was in the past a celebrated and glorious pagan center and the capital of the Persian Empire, it is there that the Antichrist will be born. It's said that he will be brought up and kept in Bethsaida and Corozain, the cities censured by the Lord in the Gospel where he says, "Woe to you, Bethsaida, woe to you Corozain!". The Antichrist will have magicians, enchanters, diviners, and wizards who at the devil's inspiration will rear him and instruct him in every iniquity, falsehood, and wicked art. Evil spirits will be his leaders, his constant associates, and inseparable companions. He will go to Jerusalem and will slay all the Christians he cannot convert to his cause under torture. He will sit on the throne of the Holy Temple, which had been destroyed, built in the past by Solomon. He will circumcise himself and will pretend that he is the son of Almighty God.

He will first convert kings and princes to him, and through them their peoples. He will destroy the places where the Lord Christ walked and the places that Lord made famous. Then he will send messengers and preachers through the whole world. His preaching and power will go from sea to sea, from East to West, from South to North. He will also work many miracles, great and never unheard-of prodigies. He will make fire come down from the sky in a frightening way, trees suddenly blossom and wither, the seas become stormy and unexpectedly calm, the elements of nature change into differing forms, change the order and flow in the water, agitate the air with winds and all sorts of commotions, and perform countless and amazing other acts, raise the dead before people to lead into mistake, if possible, even the elect. Once they see such great signs, even those who are perfect, and the God's elect ones, will doubt if he is the Christ who shall come at the end of the world according to the scriptures, or not.

Everywhere, there will be persecution against the Christians and all the elect ones. He will use three artifices against the faithful, which will be terror, money, and miracles. He will give much gold and silver to those who believe in him. Those who he cannot corrupt with money, he will overcome using terror; those he cannot overcome with terror, he will tempt seducing with signs and prodigies.

Those who he cannot seduce with prodigies, he will torture and miserably put to death before all. Then there will be such tribulation as has never been on earth since the nations began to exist. Then those who are in the field, flee to the mountains, and those who are on the roof, do not go down into his house to take anything from it[24]. Then every faithful Christian who will be found will deny God or, if he remains faithful, will perish, through sword, or a fire, or serpents, or beasts, or other kind of torture. This terrible and fearful tribulation will last for three and a half years in the whole world. The days

---

[24] *"Tunc qui in agro sunt, fugient ad montes et qui supra tectum, non descendet in domum suam, ut tollat aliquid de ea"*. This seems to be a prediction of a huge flood or a tsunami, as I explain in the introduction.

will be shortened for the sake of the elect, because unless the Lord had shortened those days, mankind would not have been saved.

(...)

Some of our learned men say that one of the Kings of the Franks will possess again the Roman Empire at the end of times and will be the greatest and the last of all kings. After ruling successfully, he will finally come to Jerusalem to lay down his scepter and crown on the Mount of Olives. This will be the end and the consummation of the Roman and Christian Empire.

According to what Paul the Apostle taught, after the end (of the Roman Empire), the Antichrist arrival will be close. And then the man of sin will be revealed, the Antichrist, who even though is a man, he will still be the source of all sins and the Son of Perdition, that is, the son of the devil, not through nature but through imitation, because he will act as the devil wants in everything, and because the fullness of diabolical power and of the whole character of evil will dwell in him in bodily fashion; where will be hidden all the values of malice and iniquity.

We spoke on his beginning, now let us explain what end he will have. This Antichrist, the devil's son and the worst master of evil, will plague the whole world for three and a half years with great persecution and will torture the whole people of God with various torments. After killing Elijah and Enoch and crowning under martyrdom the others who remain faithful, God's judgment will finally come on him, as Saint Paul wrote: "The Lord Jesus will kill him with the breath of his mouth". Whether the Lord Jesus or the Archangel Michael will kill him by the power of Jesus, he will be killed through the power of Our Lord Jesus Christ and not through the power of any angel or archangel. The doctors say that the Antichrist will be killed on the Mount of Olives upon his throne, in the place opposite to where the Lord ascended to heaven. You should know that after Antichrist has been killed, the Judgment Day will not come immediately, nor will the Lord come to judge; but as we understand from the Book of Daniel, God will grant forty *days to do penance to the elect ones because they were seduced by the Antichrist.*

How much time there will be after they complete this penitence until the Lord comes to the judgment, no one knows; but it remains in the providence of God who will judge the world in that moment in which he predetermined.

Chapter 4.

Irenaeus of Lyon

*A*uthor of *Adversus Haereses*, born between 115 and 140 in Asia Minor, he moved to Gallia, where he became a bishop of Lugdunum in Gaul, currently Lyon, France. I just included Ireneaus here because I think that most of Adso's beliefs were originated from his writings. This way, the reader can check and compare by himself.

The importance of *Adversus Haereses* ("Against Heresies") is that basically most of Middle Ages beliefs regarding the Antichrist were based on his writings. Even though scholars believe Adso took information from sources such as Pseudo-Methodius, and other sources, most of the information found in Adso's work is clearly found in Irenaeus of Lyon's writings.

Before Irenaeus, the enemy of Christ appeared with different names, and it's only after Irenaeus that the expression "antichrist" gets consistency. Later it will be used through the Middle Ages and even today.

Irenaeus uses a powerful imagination in the interpretation of some apocalyptical biblical passages found in Paul, Daniel, John's Revelation or the Apocalypse, and in other passages to develop highly original elements in his work, such as the facial aspect of the Antichrist, his miracles, his origin from the tribe of Dan, the duration of his kingdom, his enthronement in the Temple of Jerusalem etc. most of them will be adopted in the well-known medieval Adso's treaty written in the 10th century.

The following passages were translated from Latin[25] and compared to the Italian translation.

V. 25: The time (3 years and half) of Antichrist, his powers, he considering himself a "God"

"... the Temple of Jerusalem was built. It is where the Enemy will throne himself and will pretend to be Christ".
"... Half of a week means 3 years and half". (duration of antichrist' government according to his interpretation, based on Daniel's prophecies)
"He (Antichrist) having obtained all the powers from the devil will come, not as a fair king under God and the law, but as an impious and immoral king".
"He will try to be received as God."

V.30: The Antichrist comes from the tribe of Dan

"Jeremiah reveals not only that his coming will be unexpected, but it's revealed the tribe from where he will come from: 'From Dan we heard...'" (Jer 8, 16)"

---

[25] Sbaffoni, Fausto. Biblioteca Patristica. *Testi sull'anticristo. Secoli I-II.* Florence: Nardini, 1992

III. 7: The deceiving miracles he will make

"Then the impious man will be revealed, whose coming will be under the sign of Satan, through every kind of deceiving prodigy, miracle, sign, who will be destroyed by our Lord..."

Chapter 5.

Saint Malachy

---

*T*he prophecy known as Prophecy of Popes is attributed to St. Malachy (1094-1148), Latin name of Maelmhaedhoc O'Morgair, Bishop of Armagh, Ireland. In the 20th century, some books were published only about this prophecy, and everything around it is mysterious, including its authenticity and the influence it caused on Popes in the past. The St. Malachy Prophecy of Popes is only a list a names in Latin and each name would be linked to existing private information or something regarding the Popery. According to many writers, this prophecy has been fulfilled along the history and the current Pope Benedict XVI is the last Pope in the 111 Pope list, followed by a final paragraph about what seems to be the last Pope. According to my interpretation, this last pope would be the last before a reformation in the Church or, as the prophecy says, before the "end of the world".

According to some books, it seems that Saint Malachy had a vision when he was visiting the Pope in Rome in 1139, who was very concerned with the problems at that time. Malachy gave the prophecy to Pope Innocence II, who felt comforted once he saw many years to come for the Church. The prophecy would have been lost and founded in 1590 to be published in a printed book five years later.

The fact that this prophecy has remained obscure for more than 400 years is a serious element to contribute to the non-authenticity of this prophecy. Why such important prophecy written in the 12th century would become known only in the 16th century? Is this possible to happen? Maybe this prophecy was not really written by St. Malachy, it seems a clear composition. But what is amazing is that the prophecy seems to have been fulfilling, as I will explain later in this chapter. At the same time, there are some cases of prophecies that become known in printed matter centuries after they were written in manuscripts. In 1998, for example, I found a manuscript containing a prophecy attributed to St. Francis Xavier in a library in Europe. Even though I am not sure it is authentic, and it is very hard to know, I included it and it seems that it was never mentioned or printed before in any book of prophecies. In a similar manner, this prophecy may be authentic, but was printed about 400 years later its author's death.

The books published before 1595 do not mention the Malachy's prophecy. Saint Bernard, who compiled the life of the saint, who mentions some other prophecies of less importance, did not mention this one either. Especially in the 18ᵗʰ century, this prophecy was hardly criticized by some and its authenticity was not believed. In 1794 a book was published stating that there was a copy of this prophecy older than the 16ᵗʰ century copy in the Benedictine Monastery in Rimini (Italy). And at the end of the 19ᵗʰ century, some methodical refutations appeared from religious people against the non-authenticity and the prophecy regained power.

The first author who wrote something about this prophecy was the Benedictine Arnold de Wion, in his *Lignum Vitae, ornamentuem et decus Ecclesiae (Tree of Life)*, published in 1595, dedicated to Phillip II, King of Spain. He said himself that no other writer had previously mentioned the prophecy. The prophecy is a list of e 111 names in Latin, and a last paragraph regarding the last Pope. The text provided by Wion in the Lignum Vitae was the following one:

"Dunensis, Sanctus Malachias Hibernus, monachus Bencorensis et archiepiscopus Ardinacensis, cum aliquot annis sedi illi praefuisset, humilitatis causa archiepiscopatu se abdicavit anno circiter Domini 1137, et

Dunensi sede contenus, in ea ad finem usque vitae permansit. Obiit anno 1148, die 2 novembris.

Ad eum exstant Epistolae sancti Bernardi tres, videlicet 315, 316 et 317.

Scripsisse fertur et ipse nonulla opuscula, de quibus nihil vidi praeter quamdam Prophetiam de Summis Pontificibus; quae, quia brevis est, et nondum quod sciam excusa, et a multis desiderata, hica nobis apposita est.

PROPHETIA S. MALACHIAE ARCHIEPISCOPI

1. *Ex castro Tiberis.*
2. *Inimicus expulsus.*
3. *Ex magnitudine montis*

...

109. *De medietate lunae*
110. *De labore solis*
111. *De gloria olivae*

"In persecutione extrema sacrae Romanae Ecclesiae sedebit Petrus Romanus, qui pascet oves in multis tribulationibus; quibus transactis, civitas septicollis diruetur; et Judex tremendus jubicabit populum."

The last paragraph says that "In the last persecution against the Holy Roman Church, Peter the Roman will be the Pope. He will herd the flock among many tribulations, and then, the seven hill city (Rome) will be destroyed and the frightening king will judge the world".

The Pope after John Paul II (who is *De labore solis*, Labor of the Sun), has the number 111 assigned to him, and received the Latin name of "Glory to the olives". The olive trees are a symbol of the Benedictines.

The Pope Joseph A. Ratzinger, even though not a Benedictine, chose the name Benedict in honor to Saint Benedict and became Benedict XVI. This prediction that this Pope would be a Benedictine is found printed in some books of prophecies. In this case, then, it was interpreted correctly. The Pope chose the name to glorify St. Benedict.

The Church and the acceptance of this prophecy

Some Popes accepted, themselves, during their lives, the application of legends to their person. In 1670, Clemens X was in Rome where he went under an arch adorned with the motto *De flumine magno*, assigned to him in the prophecy. In Rome, to commemorate the election of Alexander VIII, a coin was embossed with his prophetical inscription: *Poenitentia gloriosa*. Other countries followed the example and coins with Malachy inscriptions appeared in many European cities to commemorate the Pope's election.

Almost all the newer books about prophecies mention the famous prophecy of Popes attributed to Saint Malachy. According to Daniel Réju in his *Les prophéties de Saint Malachie*, until the 19th century, when a restoration was done in the Basilica of Saint Paul Outside the Walls in Rome, it had 263 images that were assigned, each of them, to a Pope since Peter, in accordance with Malachy's prophecy. One of the versions of the prophecy attributed to the Monk of Padova about the Popes also matches the Malachy prophecy, but could be false.

Another coincidence is that Nostradamus used similar expressions to "work of the sun" (the same used by Malachy) referring the Pope John Paul II, even if Nostradamus work was printed 40 years before Saint Malachy's prophecy. For example, Nostradamus uses *Pol mensolée* in quatrain VIII.46; *Pol* probably referred to Poland or Paul, *solée* means sunny in French. He is probably associated to the sun because in the day John Paul II was born, there was a solar eclipse. There was another solar eclipse in the day John Paul II was buried.

In the quatrain X.29, Nostradamus used *Pol Mansol*, almost the same expression, using now the word "sun" in Latin. In the quatrain IX.85, he uses the expression "holy Paul work of the sun" in *sainct pol de Manseole* etc.

There is more than on prophecy announcing that the Church goes from Peter to Peter. Mélanie Calvat, a girl who lived in the fields of France to whom the Virgin supposedly appeared in La Salette, France, in 1846, predicted some things about the future. She said that the last Pope would be a converted Jew, as the first Peter was, what strengthens Peter II as the name of the last Pope. There are also some prophecies inscribed in old Roman catacombs in accordance with Malachy's prophecy.

There are still other prophecies about Popes, and even if many of them are without sense, found in manuscripts in libraries, some are interesting. For example, in an 16th century book I read in the National Library in France, I found a prophecy in Latin attributed to Anselm (13th century), bishop of Marsico, saying the following: "when the letter K is loved in Vatican, disgrace will come to Italy". This seems to be a reference to the Pope John Paul II, Karol Woytilla, whose name beings with a K. He was the first Pope to have a name beginning with a K. So this prophecy would be a sign that "disgrace will come to Italy". When this will happen is not clear.

Another old prophecy says that the Pope "John Obi" will be murdered. Maybe this is nothing, but *obii* means death, and some people believe John Paul I was murdered.

Other incorrect prophecies describing a list of popes, which are less known, were done in the past, but are not mentioned in books, such as the prophecies found in the manuscript *Liber prophetarum* (Bibliotheque d'Arsenal, number 50). One of them has sentences in Latin assigned to Pius II and establishes the end of the world to the seventh successor of Sistus V, around 1650. Other prophecies that appeared around 1500 are different variations of a prophecy (falsely) attributed to the Italian Abbot Gioacchino de Fiore, which is totally different of another one that was really written by him, called Prophecy of the future popes since Martin V to the Antichrist. Another false prophecy regarding the popes is the prophecy attributed to the cardinal Reginaldo, published in 1423. Other prophecies about popes became known for some time, but soon were forgotten after the non-truthfulness of them was noticed.

Chapter 6.

Father Jerome Votin

---

*T*his religious Frenchman who lived in the Monastery Saint-Germain-des-Prés, is found in a certain number of books called Jerome Botin (1358-1420) and in others as Votin. He said that he received messages in 1410 in his Monastery, in Paris. This prophecy, translated from Latin to French and here translated from French, was only known officially after 1790, when it was exhumed from documentation found in a library in a religious house. It was printed for the first time in 1830. Being a religious person, his prophecy had a extremely religious content and view, as it usually happen to prophecies done by very religious people. The final part, below, is a part of the prophecy that might be referring to our times.

"But after four centuries, Beelzebub altar's will be destroyed. The workers of iniquity will be destroyed and will die. The dew will fall from the sky over the desolated land and over the afflicted church. There will be a son with royal blood among the race of Artois. He will rule France prudently and with dignity: the spirit of the Lord will be with him; The spirit said.

Artois is a French region, which was dominated by the Spaniards and other peoples in the past.

Only after this century, there will be a shepherd who will conduct peoples in the justice and the kings in the justice. He will be honored by the princes and peoples, but before he establishes his empire, let those who did not knee before Baal to flee from Babylon (Paris?), says the Spirit.

People should think to save their lives; because the time will come when the Lord will demonstrate, through the greatness of his vengeances, the greatness of crimes with (Paris) has profaned itself. Lord will make fall over this city all the evils with which she tormented the others.

(...)

These were the words that the Spirit revealed to his Servant Jerome, who wrote them following his orders, from who the truth will be known in the due time. Amen."

Chapter 7.

Saint Césaire

---

*T*his prophecy, attributed to Saint Cesaire (born between 469-471 and dead in 542-543), Archbishop of Arles, was found in the 19th century by the Abbot Trichaud, a Dominican missionary, author of *Histoire de Saint Césaire*, published in 1853. He found the prophecy when he was looking for documentation for Saint Césaire history and, after acquiring many documents from an old family in Arles that came from the Monsieur Du Lau's library, he found a manuscript called *Magna sancti Coesarii Arelatensis archiepiscopi proedicti*, in other words, "Great prediction of Saint Césaire, archbishop of Arles". This happened in March 1847, but the prophecy was published later, because it seems that the author did not believe in its authenticity. The text of this prophecy was translated from the text in French written by the Abbot Trichaud himself after translating from Latin. Only the last section of the prophecy, reproduced below, seems to be referring to the years close to our time. Due to the long time (more than one thousand years) between Saint Cesaire's life and the time when the prediction was published, one may think the prophecy probably is not authentic. It should be noticed that the prophet usually predicts things regarding the country where he or she lived, so the cities mentioned are usually or probably cities where he lived.

About the future, the prophecy says in the end:

"The eagle flies for the second time and brings the war from the other side of France. All the scourges caused by the Almighty fall over the impious men.

All the elements are disarranged. The land shakes in many places and swallow the living ones. The fruits of the soil diminish. The roots have their humidity removed. The seeds do not produce anything. The air is corrupted and its natural direction is changed almost everywhere. Because of pestilential illnesses, a sudden and varied mortality attacks men and animals.

(...)

Who is this boastful king with rage, coming from the South with a big army? He destroys and purifies the unfaithful France to her God and to her princes.

Weakened and abandoned, the eagle drops the scepter from its weak claws and disappears forever.

Terrible noise of weapons!

The iron and the fire involve the Babylon of Gallia (Gallia is currently France), that falls in the huge fire, drowned in blood.

After that, the second city of the kingdom and another one are destroyed.

Lyon and Marseile seem to be the 2nd and the 3rd cities, according to my interpretation based on other prophecies.

Then the light of the divine mercy, because the supreme justice surprised all the wicked. The noble in exile arrives, the predestined of God. He sits on the throne of his ancestors, that the malice of depraved men had taken. He recovers the crown of the reflourished lily (the lily is the symbol of the French monarchy). Thanks to his invincible courage, he destroys the sons of Brutus (Muslims), which memory will be erased forever (as it is in the Muslim prophecies). After he establishes his kingdom in the pontifical city (Avignon, French city where the Popes lived for 70 years, future capital of France, according to some prophecies, turned into capital during the war for reasons of protection), the King puts the pontifical tiara over the head of a Holy

Pope, full of sorrows caused by the tribulations, who will oblige the clergy to live in accordance to the discipline of the first disciples. Both, united in heart and soul, will change the world. Oh, what a sweet peace! His fruits will grow until the end of times. Amen".

Chapter 8.

Orval

---

*F*or some, the prophecy of Orval was published for the first time in 1544 in old French. For others, it only became known for the first time in 1792. It was attributed to a religious man who lived in the Abbey of Orval (Aurea vallis, Golden valley, Or-val), in Luxembourg, near to the French border. According to the some prophecy books, this prediction became known only at a night in the end of the 18ᵗʰ century, when it was read by an abbot to many listeners. At that moment, the prophecy was partially copied by some people. This omission explains the mutilation of the text, of which only the second section is known. The prophecy was printed for the first time in 1829. In the 1840s, it was known as *"Forecasts revealed by God to a lonely man for the consolation of children of God"*. It is also supposed that these predictions came from Richard-Olivier (Richardus Olivarius), bishop and then cardinal, who died in 1470.

The following text was translated from the prophecy in French, from the Abbot Curicque book, who found it in the book written by Abbot Lacombe, who had access to it thanks to Marquis of Sudrie. Abbot Lacombe, writer of important books of prophecies in the 19ᵗʰ century in France, did researches on request of the archbishop of Bordeaux to determinate the authenticity of this prophecy. Abbot Curicque was also one of the most important researchers and writers in this matter in France in the 19ᵗʰ century. In the text below, only the final section, the one regarding what seems to be our times is included. There are small variations to this prophecy, which was printed differently in some books. The prophecy begins with Napoleon and finishes with the Great Monarch.

"Wow to you, big city (Paris)! Here are the kings armed by the Lord; but the fire has already destroyed you until the ground (the city will be destroyed by its citizens, probably Muslims, not by the enemies). The fair people, however, will not die. God has heard them. The sinful place is purified through fire. The big river (Seine) conducted waters reddened with blood to the sea. And France, now disintegrated, is going to regain life.

God loves peace! Come, young prince, get out from the island of your captivity. Unite the lion to the white flower, come! The old blood of centuries will finish with long discords.

Then in France it will be seen only one shepherd. The powerful man, helped by God, will establish himself well. Many wise laws will restore the peace. One will think that God is with him, so prudent and wise the descendant of the Capets will be.

Thanks to the father of mercy, the Holy Church sings again in its temples, only one great God. Many lost sheep will drink in the living river. Three princes will eliminate the cloak of mistake and will understand the faith of God. (conversion of 3 European countries) At this time, two-thirds of a great nation in the sea (might be England) will be converted to true belief.

God is blessed again during 14 times 6 moons and 6 times 13 moons. God is sad to see his mercy dissipated, however, he wishes to extend the peace, for 10 times 12 moons, thanks to the good people.

According to these numbers, there will be 282 moons of peace. Counting that each moon cycle has 28 days, it will be approximately 21 years and half of peace after what seems to be the third war. If we consider approximately 30 days for each moon, there would 23 years of peace.

This last part seems to be based on the catholic traditional prophecies:

"Only God is great! The things good are finished, the holy people will suffer.

The evil man (Antichrist) comes from two classes and grows. The white flower (the king) is darkened during 10 times 6 moons and 6 times 20 moons and disappears to appear no more. A lot of cruelty, goodness is rare in this time. Many cities will die through fire. Then, finally, Israel will come to Christ God. The cursed sects and the faithful people will be in two separated parts. But it's done: Only God is truth and one third of France and another third and half will not have faith anymore, so as the other peoples. And then more 6 times 3 moons and 4 times 5 moons and everything is separated, the final century (time) begins. After a small number of moons, God fights through his two fair men (Elijah and Enoch) and the evil man wins. But everything is over: the Almighty places a wall of fire which darkens my understanding and I can't see anymore. May He be blessed forever! Amen!"

Chapter 9.

Saint Hildegard

---

*H*ildegard (1098-1179) was born in Bermesheim, daughter of a noble family. When she was 8, her fathers offered her to God as a tithe and trusted her to Jutta von Spannheim, the only person whom Hildegard told her visions. Jutta would share the secret with Volmar, Monk at Disibodenberg, later Hildegard's secretary. Near Bingen, as a benedictine Abbess, she received in 1141 the divine order to write her visions from above. She didn't obey and then she got ill and considered her illness as a punishment. Then, helped by Volmar, she begins to write Scivias in 1141 and finishes it in 1151. In her works containing visions and prophecies - *Scivias* ("Know the paths" or "Book of visions") and *Liber Divinorum Operum* ("Book of the divine works") - Hildegard, who is better known as Hildegard of Bingen, predicted many facts about the future of humankind, some of them fulfilled, about wars and other predictions, such as about the Great Monarch, the Holy Pope, a time of peace and the antichrist, not yet fulfilled. She founded later a monastery in Rupertsberg (1148-1150), where she died in 1179. It seems that so far *Scivias* was totally translated only to German and French, and in 1990 into English.

About the wars (from *Liber Divinorum Operum*):

"When the fear for God is forgotten, wild and cruel wars will break out, many people will die and many cities will turn into a lot of ruins.

About the Great Monarch:

"Peace will come back to Europe when the white flower (Bourbon: the great king) occupies again the French throne. During this time of peace, people will be not allowed to carry weapons and the iron will be used only to allow improvements in the agriculture and as tools.

In those times, there will be many prophecies from many wise people. These will understand completely the secrets of the prophets, as well as the hidden sense of other books in the holy scripture. Their sons and daughters will prophesy as predicted before."

About the peace after the war and the natural catastrophe (from the *Liber Divinorum Operum*):

"As it was since the beginning of the world, Lord will give back to our enemies the iron rod designed to revenge with cruelty our iniquities. But when the society will be completely purged from these tribulations, the men tired of so many horrors will come back faithfully to the practice of justice and will be faithfully under the laws of the Church, that make them so pleasant to God, with the fear for God. The consolation will then substitute the desolation; so as the new law came after the old law, as the days of cure will make the anguishes of ruins be forgotten for their prosperity. (...) During this moment of renewal, justice and peace will be reestablished by decrees, so new and so unexpected, that the peoples delighted with admiration will highly confess that nothing similar was seen until this time. This world peace (will come) before the last times (times of tribulation of Antichrist) (...) and there will be justice between men and women as it was announced in the name of the Almighty by the prophet, his servant (Isaiah 4,2) saying: 'At this time, what the Lord will sprout the honor and the glory, and the land will produce happiness for the survivors of Israel"

About the Antichrist (*Scivias*, vision XI, part III). In this vision, God speaks to Hildegard. The vision seems to be based on the traditional belief, including the coming of the 2 witnesses near to the end:

"The crazy homicide, i.e., the Son of Perdition, will reign for a short period of time. The same way a day goes when the sun sets, when the last times arrive, the world will lose its power. Oh my faithful ones, listen to this witness and understand with devotion in your prudence, so that with this knowledge, the terror caused by this son of perdition does not come closer and does not precipitate you in the ruin of infidelity and perdition.

Arm yourselves and, warned by the most right signs, get ready for the most difficult combat. In effect, when the time arrives and, in a horrible way, this very evil and deceiving one will come, the mother who shall put this deceiver full of vices on the world will have been fed, since her childhood to her youth, through the devil's cunnings, in the low desert, among the most criminal men, their parents will know her poorly and they won't know with whom she spends her time anymore; in effect, it is the devil who persuades her to go here and there (...) And then, in this scalding ardor of fornication, she conceives the son of the perdition, without knowing the man from where the seed which engendered her came.

But Lucifer, the old serpent, happy with this shame, blows with all his forces on this embryo, with my permission (...) and it is this way that the son of the perdition is fed by the devil's stratagems to his maturity (...) When he arrives to a certain age, he will teach a deceiving doctrine openly (...) because as the devil said in the beginning: "I will be like Almighty" and he fell from the sky, in the same way I allow this same devil to fall in the last days, when he will say: 'I am the savior of the world'. As all the generations of followers knew that Lucifer was a liar, when in the beginning of the days, he wanted to be like God[26], in the same way, all faithful ones shall see that this son of iniquity is a liar, because before the last day, he will want to be like God. Because he is an amazing beast, he will kill all who deny him, he will form an alliance with the kings, the dukes, the princes and the rich ones, ridiculing the humility and exalting the pride, submitting the whole world to his power due to his diabolical actions.

---

[26] Belief based on the Catholic tradition or on apocryphal literature

The Son of Corruption and Ruin will appear and will reign for a short period of time, at the end of the days of the life of the world - he will come in the last days of the world. (...) His mother, a prostitute, will declare that she doesn't know his father's identity and she will state that his son was introduced by God in a supernatural way. (...) The Antichrist will come from a land between two seas and he will practice the tyranny in the east. After his birth, false teachers and doctrines will appear, following for wars, hunger and plagues. (...) When he becomes an adult, he will present a hostile doctrine to the religion, granting pardon of the sins, asking the people to believe in his divinity. He will reject the baptism and the Gospel. He will say that Jesus was a deceiver and he is not the Son of God. (...) He will say "I am the savior of the world". He will try to convince mainly the Jews that he is the expected Messiah based on the Jewish writings and the Jews will accept him. (Prophecy of Christ on this: I came on behalf of God and they didn't accept me, it will come other in his/her own name and they will accept him/it) (...) He will state that he is God who created the world, he knows the men's thoughts, that he is fair, and he will reward those who follow their teachings and will punish the ones who believe that he is not the Messiah. (...) He will preach free love and will cut of family bows. He will condemn the humility and will say that what is known traditionally as error and sin is not a sin. (...) The Antichrist sign will be an infernal symbol of baptism (...) Those who don't carry this symbol on the body will not buy nor sell. (...) He will destroy those who do not accept his faith, finally, he will dominate the whole earth. (...) The Antichrist will try to increase his miracles. Their disciples will make such miracles to torment the Christians that the people will think that the Antichrist is God. (...)

As his power extends to the wind, it will seem that he will agitate the air, to throw fire and explosions in the sky, the land will move, the mountains will be leveled, the water will rise the river against the normal flow, produce thunders, rays and hail, remove the leaves from the trees and give them again to the trees. He will deceive several types of the creatures, on the humor, the virility and the thirst. But on men, the same way, he doesn't stop exercising his maneuvers. How? He will send disease to the healthy men, the health to the ill people, he will expel the demons and he will sometimes resuscitate the dead. How? When the moment of a life to fade whose soul is under the devil's power arrives, he produces the appearance, with my permission, of illusions around of the corpse, as if it were alive, what is allowed to him to do for a very brief moment and not for a long time, due to fear that the glory of God is ridiculed by an excess in this domain. When seeing this, some will trust him, while others that will see will keep the previous faith and will avoid him. Seeking a doctor and not finding one, they appeal to him, trying to find out if he can cure them. And when he sees them, he removes the disease that he had given, and then, they love him and more and more they believe him. It is this way that many are lost because they avoid to look inside them to see their interior eyes, with which they should have looked at me (...) despising the invisible things that should be understood by the true faith.

It is this way that the Son of Perdition operates his mistakes of skills on the elements, making to appear beauty, sweetness and softness, in accordance with the wish of men which he deceives. But this power was allowed because the followers want, with their true faith, that no power exist over the good people, but only the eternal death exists over the evil ones. Everything that this son of the perdition makes, he makes for the power, pride and cruelty, without mercy, humility, prudence, but thanks to his actions and to a deep numbness, he impels men to follow him.

But I will send two witness, Enoch and Elijah, that I reserved for these times. Their mission will be to fight the man of evil and to put those who he will have seduced back on the road of the truth. They will have the virtue of operating amazing miracles, in everywhere where the son of the perdition will have spread his wicked doctrines. If on one side, I will allow this wicked one to kill them, in heavens I will give them the reward for their works.

When the Son of perdition has accomplished all his projects, he will gather their believers and he will say that he wants to arise to the sky. In the moment of this same rising, a blow of a ray will make him fall and he will die. The mountain where he will settle down to operate his rising will be covered instantly with a cloud that will spread an unbearable and truly infernal odor *of corruption. In front of his rotten corpse, a great number of people will open the eyes and will see their miserable mistake. After the son of the perdition defeat, my Son's Wife, that is the Church, will shine with an unique glory and the victims of the mistake will speed up to reenter in the fold. Concerning the day, after the Antichrist's fall, when the world shall finish, man should not try to know. The father kept the secret. Oh men, be ready for the judgment!"*

Chapter 10.

Jean de Roquetaillade

*F*rench Dominican Monk who died in 1365, he is mentioned in books of prophecies as Jean of Rochetaillade or Roquetaillade, but also as Rocketaillade or Roche-Fendue. He is also named Iohannes or Johannes of Rupescissa (Latin name), John of Cleft Rock, Giovanni di Rupescissa, Juan of Rocatalhada and with other names. Not all of the writers notice that John of Cleft Rock and Giovanni di Rupescissa were the same person, especially if the book does not give many information about the prophet. Some books of prophecies also present incorrect information concerning the time when he lived. He spent some time in the prison of Avignon, where he composed a large part of his works.

As it seems, Rupescissa or Roquetaillade died in 1365 and with his writings he became, beside the writings by Saint Hildegard, Gioacchino di Fiore and the prophecies attributed to Merlin, one of the prophecy researcher who most influenced Medieval Europe in the decades following his death. Roquetaillade wrote his works on prophecies, some of them lost, based on interpretation of prophecies, visions and older books of prophecies. His first known treaty was the *Liber (futurorum) secretorum eventuum*, a work finished in the prison in Avignon in November 1349. In this study, Roquetaillade made incorrect interpretations, assigning Babylon to Avignon[27], he studied prophecies

---

[27] French city where the Popes settled down for 70 years and the future French capital during a future world war, when Paris will be destroyed, according to the many prophecies.

on the Great Monarch who he believed that would reign in Jerusalem, prophecies about a king of the East, the Angelic Pope (French), he believed in a thousand years between the Antichrist's death and the final judgment etc. In 1356, Roquetaillade finished writing the *Liber Ostensor* (or the book revealing the times of the end of the world), also while prisoner in the Palace of Popes in Avignon, a work analyzing old prophecies as those written by Saint Hildegard, Abbot Gioacchino di Fiore, Pseudo-Methodius, Sybil of Eritrea, Pseudo-Cyril and others, with incorrect interpretations as it usually happens. His best-known work was *Vade mecum in tribulacione,* and we know this because many translations in the manuscript form were done in the Medieval Europe. Besides these 3 works, *Commentum in Oraculum beati Cyrilli* and *De oneribus orbis*; all these five books were written between 1345 and 1356 and they announced tribulations for the years 1360-1365 that didn't happen. The Antichrist, the Great Monarch and the saint Pope should appear, according to Rupescissa, in the 14th and 15th centuries. Among the lost books written by the author, there is *Festiloquium* (a book on the Antichrist) and the *Liber clavis finalium temporum.* (The book of the key of the end of the times).

Rupescissa didn't consider himself a prophet, only a discoverer of the hidden secrets in the texts. In several occasions he predicted an ecclesiastical schism as one of the signs of proximity of the end of the world. Some prophetic passages of their books seem true prophecies, if the dates associated to the events are not taken into account:

"Near to the end of the world, the Pope and the Cardinals will have to flee from Rome to a place where they will be unnoticed, under difficult circumstances. He will die in a cruel way in his exile. The sufferings of the Church will be bigger than in any past moment of its history. (...) The white eagle, following an order of the Michael the Archangel, will expel the crescent (the Muslims) of Europe where there will only be Christians. (...) An era of peace and prosperity will begin for the world. There won't be schismatic people. The Lamb will reign and the happiness of the human race will begin. Happy they will be those who escape from the risks of that terrible time,

because they will feel the taste of the fruit for Holy Ghost kingdom and the humanity's sanctification, that will be accomplished only after the death of the black eagle."

About the Angelical Pope:

"God will raise a Pope with a very holy life so that the angels will be admired. Illuminated from the high, he will reform the priesthood, will remember the apostles' life and will almost transform the whole world for his sanctity and will lead everyone to the true faith. (...) Everywhere, again people will believe in God, in virtue, in good acts. He will re-guide to the fold all of the lost sheep and there will be on earth only one faith, one law, one baptism and one same life. (...) All of the men will be friends and they will make good deeds and there won't be disagreements and wars anymore."

About the Antichrist's birth, there is this old prophecy:

"Because it was said that twenty centuries after the incarnation of the Verb, the Beast would also be embodied and she would threaten the earth with evils as impressive as the graces brought by the divine incarnation."

Chapter 11.

Abbot Gioacchino di Fiore

Calabrian, this Cistercian Monk (1130-1202) retired himself in Corazzo Abbey and later founded a religious order and a monastery. In *Divina Commedia*, Dante describes him as a prophet with a "bald and round head, aquiline nose and challenging look." He is mentioned in some books of prophecies as abbot "Merlin", Joachim or Gioacchino. Gioacchino of Fiore wrote books trying to understand old prophecies that had a great repercussion at his time. Many of his prophetic conclusions or statements were incorrect and they were objected later, as the millennialism, though. Gioacchino or Joaquin had a historical approach of the world events and divided the time in three ages, and he announced that the third age, the Holy Ghost Age or Kingdom, would begin between 1200 and 1260 and would last 1000 years long, finishing with the end of the world. In this third age, according to Gioacchino himself, the Church won't possess anything, it will live in very spiritual way, something that didn't happen in the period suggested by him. There is also a book that was widely printed in the 16th century attributed to him with prophecies similar to Saint Malachy's prophecy, where there are several illustrations on Popes, including the Angelical Pope and a "Black Pope", which is sometimes understood as a Antipope and sometimes as a Dominican. The 4th Lateran Council condemned several writings of Gioacchino. The ideas found in Gioacchinism or Joaquinism, combated by Saint Thomas Aquinas later, condemned by the Arles Council (1260) and pursued by the Inquisition, however, have been studied until our time. Joaquim of Fiore believed that he had been inspired by the Holy Ghost himself between

1190 and 1195. This inspiration helped him to interpret correctly the Apocalypse, according to him. However, certainly, he made use of extrabiblical prophecies in his texts and he misinterpreted several passages or older prophecies. For instance, he believed that the Antichrist had already been born while he was alive and he had been born in Rome. Soon it would take Pope's throne. This kind of interpretation (that the antichrist would sit on the Roman throne) probably helped Luther to spread his belief that the Pope was the Antichrist[28]. According to him:

"In the dawn, I woke up and I meditated about the Apocalypse written by Saint John. Suddenly, the eyes of my spirit were filled with the lucidity of the vision and it was revealed to me the execution of this book in accordance with the Old and the New Testament."

Some prophecies found in his writings:

"After many long sufferings supported by the Christians, and after a great bloodshed, the Lord will give peace and happiness to the destroyed nations. A notable Pope will occupy the pontificated throne, under the angels' special protection. Holy and full of kindness, he will undo all of the mistakes, and will restore the states of the Church and will unite the temporal powers exiled. He will be reverenced by all the peoples and will restore the kingdom of Jerusalem. As only Shepherd, he will unite the Eastern Church to the Western Church and there will be only one faith. The holiness and the benevolence of this Pontiff will be such that all of the potentates will bend before his presence. This holy man will squeeze the arrogance of the religious schism and the heresy. All the men will return to the primitive Church and there will be only one shepherd, one law, one master - humble, modest and fearful to God. The true God of the Jews, our Lord Jesus Christ, will make all the things prosper besides all human hopes, because God alone will heal humanity's wounds (...).

---

[28] In *Tischreden* (Table Talk), Luther wrote that the Antichrist was a existing at his days and was composed by the Pope and the Turk (Muslims) and he calculated a day for the end of the world. Luther died about 12 years before the end of the world he estimated in *Tischreden*.

This new Pope will be a shepherd and a reformulator. Thanks to him, the East and the West will be in total concordance. Babylon city (Paris?) will then be the guide and leader of the world. Rome, weakened in its temporal power, will keep its spiritual power forever and will enjoy great peace. In these happy days, the Angelic Pope will be able to send prayers full of sweetness to Heaven. The dispersed nation (Jews) shall also enjoy peace. Six and a half years after this time the Pope will surrender his soul to God. The end of his days will arrive in an arid province, located between a river and a lake close to the mountains...

In the beginning, in order to obtain happy results, needing assistance to rule, this holy Pope will ask for the cooperation of the generous French monarch. In this time, a beautiful monarch, will come as a pilgrim to witness he splendor of this glorious Pontiff, whose name will begin with the letter R."

About the Antichrist:

"Near the end of the world, the Antichrist will ruin the Pope and will usurp his Cathedral."

Rupe veni inculta, nec lænis pascua campis
   Nunc pateant, animal dulce pande ferox.
Vrbis successus turbani es cuncti, trucesq;
   Eueniant, nato belua sæua votet.

Roma tuis lacrymis totus iam personat orbis
   Hoc tamen ipsi vides læta vigere pios.
Se tibi iam magno fulgens demittit Olympo,
   En Deus, omnipotens, porrigit atq; manus.

Species Cœli in visione Gloriæ, Ecclesiast. Cap. 43.

PROFETIE

DELL'ABBATE GIOACHINO.

E T

DI ANSELMO VESCOVO DI MARSICO,

Con l'imagini in diſſegno, intorno a' Pontefici paſſati,
e c'hanno à venire.

Con due Ruote, & vn'Oracolo Turchesco, figurato sopra simil materia.

Aggiontoui alcuni marauiglioſi Vaticinij, & le Annotationi del Regiſelmo.

Conſecrati al Molto Reuerendo Padre Maeſtro

PIETRO MARTIRE RVSCA

NELLA CITTA', E DIOCESE DI PADOA

Vicario Generale della Santiſſima Inquiſitione, e Teologo dell'Eminentiſſimo,
e Reuerendiſſimo Signor Cardinale CECCHINI,

IN VENETIA, Preſſo Chriſtoforo Tomaſini. M DC XLVI.

Con Licenza de' Superiori.

Cover of an edition printed in Venice in 1646

Chapter 12.

Saint Brigita (or Brigitte)

*F*rom a noble family, Brigita (1303-1373), married the young prince Ulf Gudmardsson and became the future Queen of Sweden. Returning from a pilgrimage, her husband died and she refused to have a role in the Swedish court and she decided to live in a monastery. There, she believed to receive revelations from saints and Mary about future subjects such as the final judgment, which she wrote in eight volumes, and called *Revelations* (*Revelationes cœlestes seraphicæ Matris sanctæ Birgittæ*). In spite of her good faith and mercy, Brigita was accused of having a wide imagination and her supposedly prophetic texts had mistakes. She tried to convince the Swedish King to go in a Crusade to convert Russia, she later established a new religious order and finally died returning from a pilgrimage to Jerusalem.

There is a strange prophecy that is said to have been found in a box in the sepulcher of the Benedictine Priests in Naples and it was attributed to her. She would have stated that there would be big problems in the world every time that Saint Mark's party matched Easter, Saint Antoine's Pentecostes and Saint John party with Corpus Domini. These parties coincided in 1791, when the French Revolution happened. Also in 1848 (time of revolutions in Europe), 1859, 1886 and 1943, time of the Second War. However, the remaining of the prophecy seems incorrect.

They were also predictions attributed to Saint Brigita assigned to years probably not predicted by her, at least they are not contained in her revelations. If these prophecies were really written or said by her, they are many incorrect. For 1848, she predicted "people against people", time when many revolutions happened in Europe and in the Church, when Pope Pius IX had to leave Rome. The last year foreseen by the saint is 1999, when "the lights will fade out". The only important thing that happened in 1999 that could be related to the future is the arrival of Vladimir Putin in power, it seems to me. On the other hand, there are texts stating that she predicted that in 1890 there would be "only one shepherd and one flock", what didn't happen. Another prophecy, very similar the this, consists of a list of years associated to sentences that were not fulfilled, supposedly also found in the sepulcher of a monk in a monastery in Naples, with years also wrongly matched, where in 1900 the lights would fade out. Probably forged by another monk of bad nature, the style is highly similar to the prophecies above attributed to Saint Brigita.

The conversion of the unfaithful people was revealed to Saint Brigita several times. Here is an important passage, as revealed to her by Jesus Christ:

"Know that a time will come when the converted pagans will give such devotion examples that the Christians will be, in some way, servants of them in the spiritual life: then that passage of the Holy Books will become true: that I will be glorified by the people who didn't know me. (...) All men together will sing: Glory to the Father, to the Son and to the Holy Spirit, and may all the saints of the Heavens be praised".

Once she was in ecstasy and she heard Jesus Christ talking about the Greeks, at the end of the times:

"Concerning the Greeks, they know that all the Christians need to keep the only Catholic faith and to submit themselves to the Roman Church, they also know that my only Universal Vicar in the whole world, the Sovereign Roman

Pontiff, exercises the spiritual power over them. Even this way, they don't want to be subject to this Church of Rome nor to my Vicar and they reject this spiritual subjection because of their obstinate pride, for their selfishness and because of their hideous vices and other things that turn them slaves of the vanities of the world. So, they will be no mercy neither pardon in my court in their death.

According to a revelation told by Christ, the age of the world can be divided in three times. At the end of the third time, the Antichrist is born:

"At the end of this age (the third), the Antichrist will be born. As the children of God come from faithful parents to this world, in the same way, the Antichrist will be born from a cursed woman, but simulating the holiness, and from a cursed man, and from both the demon will create his work with my permission. But the Antichrist arrival (...) will happen in one time that is known by me, when the iniquity will be beyond the limits and the impiety will grow in an immense way: when 'iniquitas ultra modum abundaverit, et impietas excreverit in immensum'. Know, also, that before the Antichrist comes, the doors of the faith will be open to some nations, where the word in the scripture will be fulfilled 'a nation that doesn't know you, you will call her; and this nation that doesn't know you will run to you'. (Isaiah 55, 5) After this, when the Christians love the heresies and the iniquitous ones destroys the clergy and the justice, this will be, don't make a mistake, the sign that the Antichrist is not far. (...) Finally, the worst of men will come, who will be united to the Jews, and will make the best he can to erase the name of the Christians. Many will be dead".

INCIPIT PRIMVS LIBER

REVELATIONVM
CAELESTIVM
SANCTAE BRIGITTAE
DE SVETIA.

VERBA DOMINI NOSTRI IESV CHRISTI
AD SVAM ELECTAM SPONSAM
DILECTISSIMAM.

De certificatione suæ excellentissimæ Incarnationis; & de im-
probatione prophanationis , & fractionis fidei nostræ ,
& baptismi ; & qualiter ad sui dilectionem inuitat
præfatam dilectam sponsam.

CAPVT PRIMVM.

EGO sum Creator cæli & terræ, vnus in Deitate cum Patre & Spiritu sancto. Ego sum qui Prophetis,&Patriarchis loquebar , & quem ipsi expectabant. Ob quorum desideriū & iuxta promissionem meam, assumpsi carnem sine peccato & concupiscentia , ingrediens viscera Virginea, tanquam Sol splendens per lapidem mūdissimum. Quia sicut Sol vitrum ingrediendo non lædit , sic nec virginitas Virginis in assumptione humanitatis meæ corrupta est . Ego autem sic assumpsi carnem , vt non derelinquerem Deitatem . Et non minor eram in Deitate cum Patre , & Spiritu sancto omnia regens, & implens, licet in vtero Virginis eisem cum humanitate . Quia sicut splendor nunquam separatur ab igne, sic Deitas mea nunquam ab humanitate separata est,nec in morte . Deinde corpus ipsum mūdissimum à peccato pro peccatis omnium à planta pedis vsque ad

A

Revelationes St. Brigitta, cover of a 1628 edition, in Latin

Chapter 13.

Napoleon

*H*e conquered almost the whole Europe and died in the Saint Helene island, after the war in Waterloo in 1815. In a book published in Italy in 1935, written by Alberto del Fante[29], I found a couple of prophecies attributed to Napoleon. According to the book, when Napoleon could not beat Russia in 1812, because of the English opposition, he would have predicted:

"England will pay for this, Russia will destroy England and will be the scourge of Europe."

When Napoleon was sent to Saint Helene island, he predicted the following referring to England and Venice, the last one a Republic at that time:

"You, England, will die as the superb republic of Venice."

Napoleon was very interested in prophecies, and it seems that when his army found an old manuscript with oracles in Egypt, he ordered the translation and only him had access to the translation.

In the book *Napoleon Prophète*, printed in 1849 and in 1850 in Paris, some other prophecies can be found. For example, before dying in Saint Helene island, he would have said:

---

[29] Del Fante, Alberto. *Le Procellarie del Futuro*. Bologna: Galleri, 1935

"Within fifty years, Europe will be Republican or Cossack".

NAPOLÉON PROPHÈTE,

ALMANACH DU

PETIT CAPORAL.

1850   1850

Prix : 10 centimes.

PARIS,
RUE DES GRAVILLIERS, 25, ET RUE SAINT-JACQUES, 41.

Cover of a 1850 book with Napoleon prophecies

Chapter 14.

Savonarola

---

*J*erome (or Girolamo in Italian) Savonarola was born in Ferrara in 1452, son of noble parents, and the third of seven sons and daughters[30]. At the same year, the Emperor Frederic III came down to Italy with 2000 men in direction to Rome (through Ferrara) to take the Imperial crown. In 1453, Constantinople fell under the Muslim power and there was a general apocalyptic fear in Europe that the Muslims could rule over Europe. Luther had used the "Muslim fear" to calculate that the end of the world was not far.

In 1475 Savonarola decided to enter in a cloister, after listening to a preaching the previous year. Savonarola spent 7 years in the St. Dominic Monastery in Bologna. The corruption of those times had led him to close himself in cloister, where he could feel well in his prayers in solitude.

After the death of Pius II (1464), a scandalous corruption in the Popery begun, which would reach its summit with the Spaniard Alexander VI. Sistus IV, who had sat on the throne in 1471 was avid for gold, and spent a lot of money. Everyone knew that he had acquired the

---

[30] Most of what is written in this chapter was taken from *La Storia di Girolamo Savonarola* (more than 1000 pages in 2 volumes), written by Pasquale Villari, printed in 1839 in Florence by Felice Le Monnier. I also visited the library of Ferrara in Italy, where I checked *Profezie Politiche e Religiose di Fra Hieronymo Savonarola ricavate dalle sue prediche da Messer Francesco de'Guicciardini l'Historico*. Florence: Cellini, 1863

right to be a Pope paying for the vows and giving positions in exchange of it.

This way the Savonarola years went by. He visited Florence and preached there for the first time in 1491 menacing the wrongdoers against future scourges. The people gathered to listen what he had to say. His hard words didn't pleasant Lorenzo the Magnificent, from the Medici family, the famous noble family who ruled the city at those times and Lorenzo sent five important people to talk to him and ask him to control his mouth and his words. Savonarola didn't receive well these five men and said: "I see that you came because you were sent by Lorenzo. Tell him to do penitence for his sins, because the Lord does not spares anyone and is not afraid of the princes". Naturally the Medici family did not like the answer and Savonarola was not welcome in Florence anymore.

According to *Archivio Storico*, published by Father Marchese, Savonarola predicted the following in 1494, assigning the coming of the French people to the end of times, which I translate from Old Italian:

Soon each tyrant shall be seen submerged
And the whole Italy shall be soon conquered
With its shame, vituperation and damage.
Rome, you shall soon be gained;
I see coming onto you the knife of wrath
The time is at hand and each day flies
My Lord wants to reformulate the Church
And convert each barbaric people
There shall be one shepherd and one sheepfold
But before this, the whole Italy will be ill
And so much blood on this will flow
That a rare happening this will be for all its people

Sermons like these conquered a so large interest so that Florence cathedral was crowdy everyday when Savonarola was preaching. Savonarola had become the most important person in Florence, at that time, a Republic.

Inviting the French people to invade Italy, Savonarola was against the Medici family, as was the public opinion, and slowly the people in Florence. In 1494, the Medici family members were expelled from Florence and Savonarola had become the only man in those days who could command the people of Florence, because the people listened to him more than to any other. When the Medici left Florence, he preached that the sword had come and the prophecies had been fulfilled and the sins of Florence, Rome and Italy were the cause of that hard moment. This happened when Charles VIII and other Frenchmen invaded Florence and asked for a sum that the citizens could not pay.

When the French people left Florence, Savonarola proposed a new form of government, suggesting a government similar to the "Consiglio Grande" (Great Council) of the people of Venice, giving his first steps in the politics.

"Oh my people! You know that I never wanted to go in the state affairs: do you believe that I would like to do it, if I didn't see that this is necessary to the health of souls?"

The voice and suggestion of the priest was towards freedom. It's the opinion of many historians that without the suggestion of Savonarola, the decision would be different, but his suggestion for the *Consiglio Grande* in Venice style was accepted. So Savonarola had instituted a new government in the state of Florence.

Savonarola suggested laws and played an important role in the politics in Florence at that time. Later Machiavel will consider him only a cunning and astute priest.

From this time, the Medici tried to go back to Florence, using the army. At the same time, the Pope, very corrupt and highly interested in politics, power and lands at that time, had obliged Savonarola to keep silence and do not preach for some time. He would be later tortured for weeks in Florence during the process ordered by the Pope in Rome. They used the torture of *fune* (a kind of rope), which was used to obtain anything under confession. The process involved three aspects: religion, politics and prophecy. Savonarola was considered innocent three times, from the beginning to the end of the 3 processes, and even though nobody signed to state this, this information was hiddenly spread in Italy.

Although innocent, the prosecutors decided for the death of Savonarola and on May 23rd, 1498 he was burned in a fire.

His prophecies were basically about the conversion of all peoples into the Catholicism, and a reformation in the Church after big problems, and these things would soon happen. He also predicted political events, such as the expulsion of the Medici in Florence and the invasion of the French people, both happened in his lifetime. In 1497, he wrote *De veritate prophetica, Dialogus* (Dialogue about the prophetical truth), where he tried to analyze scientifically how a person can know the future, through a vision, dream etc. He also wrote another text about prophecy, called *Compendium Revelationum*, published in 1495. In this last one, it's possible to find his main visions.

In his sermons, found in *Profezie Politiche e Religiose*, published in 1863, I selected the following prophecies:

"Lord commanded me to predict the sourges. If I speak, my body will die. If I don't speak, my soul will die".
"To Saint Peter in Rome, the whores will come, it will become a pig and cattle-shed, they will drink and eat inside it etc."
"The Turks will be converted to the (catholic) faith".
"Many people will die in Italy soon, soon".
"The Church will be renewed and this will happen soon, and then the unfaithful will be converted and this will be soon".

"Oh Italy, Oh Rome. I will surrender you in the hands of other people, who will destroy you until your foundation. I will bring you so many illnesses that few people will remain. Cruel and wicked men will go over Italy and Rome".(…) The grass will grow over the city streets".

"God want to punish the whole Italy and out of Italy the whole Christianity".
"

Chapter 15.

Mother Shipton

---

*A*n important doubt that exists concerning Mother Shipton does not regard the authenticity of her prophecies, but herself. Did she really exist?[31] Some writers who visited libraries in England stated that the most famous prophecy attributed to her is false. And some of them asked if she even existed, which is the same question many make when the matter is Merlin.

She is undoubtfully the most famous prophetess in the world. And her most famous prophecy says that the world would finish in 1881. Today it is certain that this prophecy was fabricated in the 19th century it was and falsely attributed to Mother Shipton, although some writers claim that this prophecy was published in 1448 and republished in 1641, such as William Henry Harrison[32], even though the earliest mention to her existing today is found in a book printed in 1641[33], which does not have the famous 1881 prophecy. The prophecy is definitively false as many other prophecies attributed to her published worldwide seem to be. And if Mother Shipton existed, if she was born in 1488, about 40

---

[31] For more information about this matter, please see *Mother Shipton: Secrets, Lies, and Prophecies*, written by the same author of this book.
[32] Harrison, William H. *Mother Shipton: The Yorkshire Sibyl Investigated. The Result of a Critical Examination of the Extant Literature Relating to the Yorkshire Sibyl*. 1881
[33] The Prophesie of Mother *Shipton*, In the Raigne of King *Henry* the Eighth. Fortelling the death of Cardinall *Wolsey*, the Lord *Percy* and others, as also what should happen in insuing times. London, Printed for *Richard Lownds*, at his shop adjoining to Ludgate, 1641.

years after the prophecy was known as attributed to her, that is another reason to think the prophecy is probably not an authentic prophecy by Mother Shipton.

This is what William Harrison says in his book, published in 1881:

"The lines in question, and the notorious prophecy about the end of the world, were fabricated about twenty years ago, by Mr. Charles Hindley. The editor of Notes and Queries says, in the issue of that journal dated April 26th, 1873:

"Mr. Charles Hindley, of Brighton, in a letter to us, has made a clean breast of having fabricated the Prophecy quoted at page 450 of our last volume, with some ten others included in his reprint of a chap-book version, published in 1862."

Most of the precise details in Chapter I, about the birth, life and death of Mother Shipton, are fabrications which have been reproduced time after time in chap-books. There is no absolute evidence that any one of the details is true, but there may be some foundation for the incident narrated about Cardinal Wolsey".

So, the "supposed facts" such as her name, etc. are probably false. Many books will teach her name was Ursula Sonthiel, and that she lived in Skipton, place that might have been called Shipton, in the past in England. She would have been born in 1488 in Yorkshire, got married when she was 24 with a carpenter who lived in Skipton. She probably died in 1561 after predicting her own death. According to some books, near the towns of Clifton and Skipton, there was a stone with the following inscription:

Here ly's she who never ly'd
Whose skill often has been try'd
Her Prophecies shall still survive,

And she keep her name alive.

The 1881 prophecy was published with variations in the 20th century. According to some, this prophecy was published in 1448 under the title "Ancient Prediction" and was later attributed to Mother Shipton. It is also possible that the end of the prophecy has been added to the prophecy later.

ANCIENT PREDICTION
Supposedly published in 1448, and supposedly republished in 1641[34].

Carriages without horses shall go,
And accidents fill the world with woe.
Around the world thoughts shall fly
In the twinkling of an eye.
The world upside down shall be
And gold be found at the root of a tree.
Through hills man shall ride,
And no horse be at his side.
Under water men shall walk,
Shall ride, shall sleep, shall talk.
In the air men shall be seen,
In white, in black, in green;
Iron in the water shall float,
As easily as a wooden boat.
Gold shall be found and shown
In a land that's now not known.
Fire and water shall wonders do,
England shall at last admit a foe.
The world to an end shall come,
In eighteen hundred and eighty one."[35]

---

[34] False information: the prophecy was not published in these years
[35] Even though this prophecy is not authentic, and was fabricated in the 19th century, curiously some inventions mentioned were created in the 20th century.

William Harrison says in his book: "*This, and other prophecies, said to have been copied from records of unimpeachable antiquity in the British Museum Library, which prophecies in some cases have been reproduced in alleged fac-simile, have raised curiosity even in the scientific and skeptical mind, and fanned the flame of imagination in the mind idealistic, as to what amount of truth, or error, or deception, may be at the root of the matter.*"

In fact, if the prophecy were true, it would have been printed in the 1641 book, which I have a copy and found nothing about it, except prophecies about past events, today considered of without general importance.

In Internet, a few years before the 2000, someone published the following false prophecy attributed to Mother Shipton. The prophecy was supposedly found in a manuscript in Australia and published by a local magazine. False prophecies continue to be fabricated and Internet seems to be the new media where are spread world-wide.

"*When man gets close to the last century
Three sleeping mountains unite their breath
And throw mud, ice and death
And earthquakes swallow cities and towns;
In lands for me unknown.*

(...)

*The dragon tail is only a sign
For humankind fall and decline.*"

Chapter 16.

Gonçalves Annes Bandarra

---

*T*his Portuguese man who lived in the years 1500-1566, a shoemaker born in Trancoso, left written a text disposed as quatrains that were known as quatrains of Bandarra. In 1541, the Inquisition called him to Lisbon to answer about the popular quatrains which were being spread in his name as author. Father António Vieira, who spent years writing about prophecies, wrote about him: *"Bandarra was a true prophet, because he predicted and wrote so many things, so exact, so particular, so many years before, and we saw all of them fulfilled with our eyes..."* Statements such as this one took this priest to prison where he lived for 22 months. Bandarra was very well-known in the past in Portugal and some texts said that for 200 years he was read more than the Bible.

During the 16th and 19th centuries, variations to Bandarra quatrains were created. They had originally been written by Father Gabriel João, in Trancoso village. Some of these quatrains were found in 1729 in São Pedro Church in this village. An author of a book printed in the beginning of the 19th century in London in Portuguese says that concerning the existence of Gonçalves (also called Gonçalo) Annes Bandarra, his time and the authenticity of his prophecies, well documented, there can be no doubt.

Here are some predictions attributed to Bandarra. He also predicted about the "defeated Turk".

I see a great King coming
All blessed
And he will be so successful
that he will defend the parishioners

This one will keep the Law
from all heresies
He will defeat the fantasies
Of those who keep what I don't know

I see a leader coming
From the Kingdom beyond the hills,
Wishing war
Hardworking knight.

This one will be the first
Who will put his banner
In the dragon's head
And will kill him completely.

I think that after will come
A shepherd to the sheep
Very tame and good keeper,
Who will reform the flock.

This shepherd will give to eat
a very healthy grass
And his sheep with wool
God will dress.

All will have one love
Heathens and pagans,
The Jews will be Christians,

With no mistake anymore.

They will serve only one Lord,
Jesus Christ.
All will believe, that he already came
The Anointed Savior.

Everything that is said here
Look carefully the prophecies
written by Daniel and Jeremiah
Meditate deeply on them.

One will think that on these days
There will be great news
New laws and varieties,
Thousand fights and disputes.

Among the quatrains found in 1729 divided in dreams, here are some translated from Old Portuguese:

First dream:

1st Quatrain:

In you who will be the fifth (John V)
After the second is dead
My prophecies I write down
With these letters that now I paint

2nd Quatrain:

The trunk is still to come
I already see the cedar upright

Not much goes from Peter to Peter[36]
If the foliage is measured by the trunk

6th Quatrain:

I make full quatrains
Verses very well measured
That shall be fulfilled
In the end of times

Second dream:

5th Quatrain:

This dream that I dreamt
Is the very certain truth
That from the hidden island
Will come this king.

---

[36] Catholic Church, the 1st Pope and the last one will both be called Peter, according to some prophecies

Chapter 17.

Nostradamus

---

*I*n a 1558 book, he is called Monstradamus, a word to remember a Monster, in the worst sense, where the author compared him to the old serpent, saying that he changed his prognostications "year after year". In another 16th century book, written by Laurens Videl (which we will see here), he is compared to the false prophets and other things. At the same time, in a book about Nostradamus written by Jean C. Fontbrune says that among all people who lived in the 16th century, Nostradamus (1503-1566), born in France, was the one about whom more was written after his death, more was written about him than kings, queens etc. And some people thought, as he wrote in his books, that he never made a mistake. Who could be right? Was Michel de Notredame only a deceiver, a monster?

Some people wrote that Nostradamus never committed mistakes, which is probably wrong. Even the Queen of France, Catherine de Médici, asked him to visit the palace and tell her what she expected for the future, as the old Emperors and Kings did in the past.

Many books about prophecy mention Nostradamus, but the prophecies written by him were not easy to understand and full of mysteries, and the result is that any book that tries to understand what he wrote usually (not to say always) misinterprets what he said or the future itself. The weirdest interpretations were created along the years. Even researchers who studied the prophet and his prophecies for more than ten or twenty years, such as Jean Charles de Fontbrune, misinterpret his writings.

Nostradamus most-known work was published in a book called Oracles and it is disposed as centuries, which are groups of 100 quatrains. They are usually ambiguous and very hard to understand. In fact, his prophecies are usually not understandable.

The method that Nostradamus used to know the future is described by him in the 2 first quatrains (first century), published for the first time in 1555. Many writers seem to agree that Nostradamus used an old method, which was used in the Old Egypt, found in the book called *De mysteriis Aegyptiorum* (Egypt Mysteries), written in the 4th century by Iamblicus or Jamblichus. This book was considered a work of witchcraft or magic, because it supposedly taught how to contact spirits and get information from them.

According to my viewpoint and research, the way used by Nostradamus to predict the future was a mix of old oracles found in Greece, such as Delphus (or Delphi) and Branches. It was basically a way to contact spirits, as spiritualism today preaches. Similarly, Nostradamus prophecies were called oracles by the prophet himself and were disposed in form of ambiguous quatrains, exactly as the old oracles were, as we can find in Herodotus book, for example, written in 5th BC. Nostradamus possibly had access to old books that explained how these old oracles were performed, a mystery still today for archaeology, as it is believed that he had access to old books and burned them to avoid risks related to Inquisition. But the similarities do not end here.

The Delphi oracle was visited for more than 1000 years. The In the Athena Museum, there is a bit of pottery from approximately 440 BC, which is the next image, where there is a woman (the Sybil or prophetess) sitting on a tripod, in Dalphoi, transmitting a oracle. The woman (also known as Pythia) has a basin with water in one hand and a branch in the other hand. These 3 elements (the tripod or the aerial chair, the water and the branch) are mentioned by Nostradamus in his two quatrains, in the first century, the ones he used to explain his artificial method of predicting the future. Was he a real astrologer? Did he talk to spirits? We cannot know today.

Plutarch stated that the oracle at Delphi never committed a mistake. This seems hard to believe, and Nostradamus received the same fame from some people at his time.

The Delphic Pythia had in her hands a branch, laurel, and she washed her feet or the clothes near the feet with water. Then the "god" (or spirit) spoke through her. Please see the following figure an old image representing the Greek Pythia.

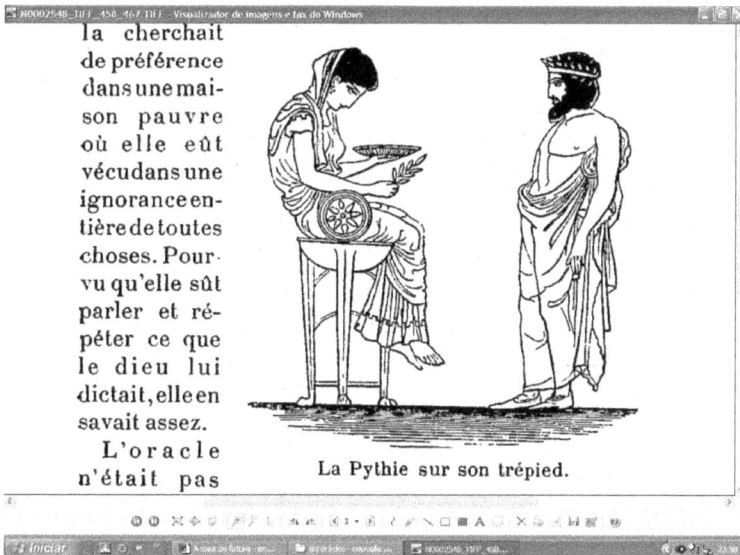

la cherchait de préférence dans une maison pauvre où elle eût vécu dans une ignorance entière de toutes choses. Pourvu qu'elle sût parler et répéter ce que le dieu lui dictait, elle en savait assez. L'oracle n'était pas

La Pythie sur son trépied.

According to Philipp Vandenberg[37], "it would be wrong to regard Didyma (or the Branches oracle) merely as a branch of Delphi. Didyma is pre-Grecian, as Pausanias testifies". Concerning Delphi, he says: "The fire was fed with pinewood and laurel branches." And "in addition to the tripod, it had to accommodate the golden statue of Apollo (God of Prophecy),

---

[37] *The Mystery of the Oracles. World-famous Archaelogists reveal the best-kept secrets of Antiquity.* New York: Macmillan Publishing, 1979

Apollo's lyre and sacred armor, the most illustrious omphalos, and several branches of laurel". "Naked, the Pythia bathed in the Castalian Spring: this served for cultic purification because the water was considered to be prophetic". "Meanwhile, the Pythia (...) sat on the tripod. (...) about three feet high (...) the second important role during the prophetic ritual was played by a laurel bush."

Nostradamus Quatrain 1 – Century 1

Alone at night in a secret study,
Alone, in a relaxed state, on an aerial chair
The flame goes out of loneliness
And makes prosper what must be believed.

Nostradamus Quatrain 2 – Century 1

The branch in the hand in the middle of Branches
With water he washes the inferior part of the cloth and the feet
A fear and a voice make tremble
Divine splendor: the divine sits close.

So the way to predict the future described by Nostradamus is highly similar, maybe the same, to the one used in old Greece, in the oracles of Delphi[38] and maybe Branches.

---

[38] A few years ago it was discovered a fissure from where gas was coming out in the island of Delphi, in the mountainous regions where the ruins of the Delphi temple are located, exactly in the chamber where the Sybil should be sitting inside the temple. After analyzing carefully the river waters, it was found out that the gas, existing still today, is ethylene. Ethylene is a sweet gas that probably caused the trance in the Delphi Sybil, as the legend said. Strabo mentioned a "vertically dug hole", from where a "vapor issues, that produces an ecstasy". According to the legend, the temple of Delphi was built in the mountains, 600 meters high, after goats breathing the gas had a strange behaviour and "spoke".

Nostradamus studied Medicine and he was a doctor for some years, even though he didn't finish University, but one day in the middle of the 16th century he decided to change career and wrote prophetical almanacs, which had a great success at that time. His fame of prophet crossed the borders of France and even the Queen Catherine de Médice visited him. After publishing the prophetical almanacs, he published the centuries or oracles, groups of quatrains. In 1555, 1557 and in 1568, after his death, these prophetical quatrains were published.

In his grave there is an inscription in Latin saying "*Here lies the man who knew the future of the world*". On the other side, even if famous and wanted by the Queen, still in his time, some people wrote that his prophetical statements were wrong. In a book published in 1558 in Avignon, France, called *Declaration des Abus, Ignorances et Seditions de Michel Nostradamus, de Salon de Craux en Provence, ouvre tresutile e profitable â un chacun* (Declaration of the abuses, ignorances and seductions of Michel Nostradamus, a very useful work for everyone) written by M. Laurens Videl, the writer states that Nostradamus was a mediocre astrologer, and that he committed basic mistakes in astrology and states that many of his predictions were not fulfilled. Here are some extracts found in this book:

Nostradamus "*seeds big mistakes through the whole world, against every rule of astrology*" and he "*wants to do predictions of almanacs which will be guides to conduct to the true principles of astrology, which he never understood*". "*Many people think today that all who do predictions or prognostics use magic and superstition.*" He says that Nostradamus knew "*the witchcraft of the evil spirits through a profane and terrestrial magic*". In a certain moment, the writer, who knew Nostradamus in person, exposed basic mistakes of astrology found in Nostradamus books saying: "*I ask you, Michel, what made you do this? If not your ignorance, being unable to know that the planets in ephemeredes are calculated at noon*

*and that the sun has entered for a long time in the first point of Aries..." And:
"Certainly, if I wanted to mention all your ignorances, abuses and stupidities
included in your works after four or five years, it would be necessary to write
a very large book, but I prefer to mention only a few. (...) You predicted that
in 1555, January, many false prophets would be seducing the people, even
though I don't know any other false prophet different of you (...) and for one
truth that is said, it is said five hundred lies (...) In the 1552 prognostic, you
say that the war, famine, sterility and death of many will happen, but
through faith all this could be avoided, and you pray so that this does not
happen. Isn't this a contradiction? Because later you say that it is necessary
that all this happen. (...) In March 1555, you say that it is the renovation of
this century, in April, there will be only one shepherd and one flock. (...) I
come back to your abuses and ignorances. In January 1555, you say that the
full moon starts on the 7th at the 6 minutes in the morning. Why do you say 6
minutes, you idiot? The full moon will start at 8 pm and not in the 6 minutes
in the morning"*

*(...) and as you predicted the death of many people, some died and others are
full of life, even here in Avignon, and there is a woman to whom you said that
in a certain month she would be dead and she fell very ill of fear. Why do you
do this evil to people? And you did the same to a priest that I know. And this
priest and this woman are full of life and if it is the will of God, they will live
more than you. (...) Where do you take your lies from? Oh intolerable
pestilence, who puts many people in error through your false doctrine, full of
abomination (...)*

*And according to your prophecies, you say that before the total end of the
world, there will be so many deluges and so many floods that there will not
exist land uncovered with water (...) even if this is against the Holy Scripture,
which we witnessed that God will make the land die through water, as it is
written in Genesis, 9. (...) And if you understood some principles of astrology,
you would know that you shouldn't have abandoned your studies to write
almanacs (...) Similarly, you say you cannot fail nor make a mistake. (...)
From Avignon, on this day that you menaced me of many evils, which is
November 21st, 1557."*

Nostradamus also wrote:

"There will be a solar eclipse darker and more tenebrous than any other since the creation of the world, except the one happened after the death of Christ. And in October there will be a translation of some degrees, in such way that one will think that the Earth has lost its natural movement and has dived in eternal darkness in the abyss. (...) This will happen after extreme changes, fallen nations and big earthquakes."

Although Mr. Laurens Videl seemed to have good reasons to write hard words about Nostradamus, he is one of the most printed prophets, maybe the most famous one not included in the Bible. The most famous prophecy written by Nostradamus is the X.72, concerning the year 1999. It is found printed in many books about the subject, and 1999 is usually interpreted as the year of a war.

This prophecy is about a "king", not about a war. It mentions the word "king" twice and it does not mention the word war anywhere. It announces the arrival of an important leader to power in 1999. If my interpretation is correct, and only the next years will answer this question, this will become the most amazing and accurate prophecy ever written by man in the whole history of mankind.

Quatrain X.72

"L'an mil neuf cent nonante neuf sept mois,
Du ciel viendra um grand Roy d'effrayeur,
Ressusciter le grand Roy d'Angolmois,
Avant après Mars regner par bonheur."

Translation:

In 1999, seven months,

From the sky a great frightening King will come

The great King of Angoulmois lives again.

Before (and) after March (2000), (he) rules for happiness.

In 1999, after seven completed months, on the 9th of August, Vladimir Putin, at that moment unknown in the international scenery, became worldly known as Prime Russian Minister. On the 31st of December of that same year, Yeltsin resigned and Putin became President of Russia. We must admit that 1999 was the year of Vladimir Putin. In the following year, in March, there were elections in Russia. Putin was already President before March and continued to be President after the elections in March. When he suddenly appeared in August 1999, Putin had 2% of approval of the population. Less than one year after, in the election of March of 2000, the Russians elected Putin as their President. Putin arrived in power in August, not in July as the prophecy says, but this depends on the calendar we use: Should we use our calendar or Nostradamus time calendar?

Nine days is the difference between the full "seven months" predicted by Nostradamus and 9th of August. This difference disappears if we realize that another calendar, the Julian calendar, was used at Nostradamus' time. Our calendar, the Gregorian calendar, began to be used a few years after Nostradamus' death. When it was implemented, ten days were "ignored" or "skipped" or "eaten": in other words, after 4th of October 1582, came the 15th. Nothing in history happened in these 10 days because they didn't even exist. Therefore, 30th of July, 1999 in Nostradamus calendar (the old Julian calendar) means 9th of August, 1999 in our calendar. What accuracy!

The expression "from the sky will come a frightening king" could mean "from the North, a frightening king will come." If you look at a map, you will see that Russia is located above France, the place where the prophecy was done.

Concerning the expression "King of Angoulmois", the King of France was a Duke at Nostradamus' time. Francis I (the first) was Duke of a region called Angouleme. Nostradamus calls Putin as King of Angoulmois for the following reasons: As Putin, Francis I is European, and Francis I tried to attack the united Europe. At that time, Charles V ruled almost the whole of Europe, and he had lands in Germany, Austria, Holland, Belgium, Hungary, Italy and Spain, and the whole Latin America, except Brazil. At a certain point, King Francis got allied with the Muslims to invade Europe. So, a European leader was allied to the Muslims to attack the united Europe.

Even though Russia is in Europe, today it is out of the European Union, as France was at Nostradamus time, in the 16th century. Each line of the quatrain is very clear, not ambiguous. These are the reasons why this prophecy seems to be predicting Vladimir Putin very accurately:

Angoulmois was a medieval province of France. This name (Angoulmois) can be found in some encyclopedias currently in use. Historically, Angoulême was the capital of Angoumois. It became a French province when the Count d'Angoulmois François (or Francis) went to the French throne and became King Francis I, in 1515. Francis I was an autocratic king and his rule was characterized by wars, according to books of history.

The term "Mars", erroneously interpreted by prophecy writers as "war" during centuries in books of prophecies, also means March, the third month. This misinterpretation of Mars caused the wrong belief that Nostradamus foresaw that the third world war would break out in 1999, which he never did, it seems. Nostradamus wasn't wrong about that, but his interpreters were, during 450 years. Anyway, as the reader could see, the quatrain X.72 seems to be related to Vladimir Putin.

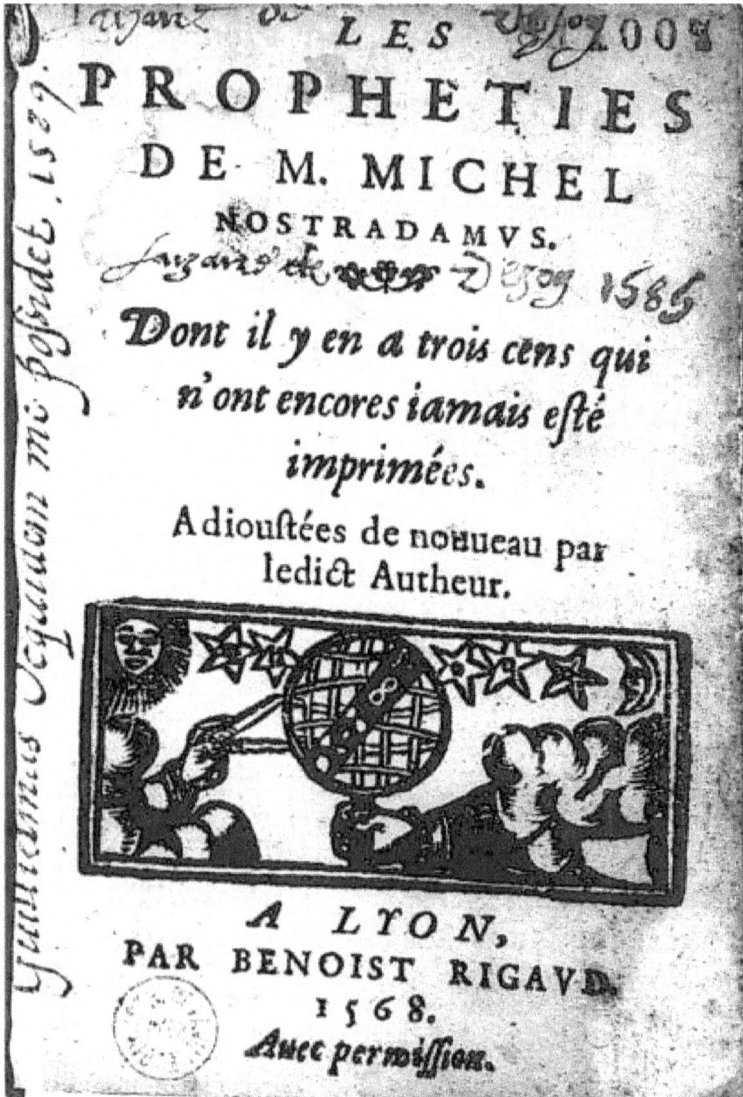

Cover of the 1568 edition

Cover of the 1668 edition

LA
PREMIERE INVE-
Étiue du Seigneur Hercules le François,
contre Monstradamus.

'Eſt a vous Princes ma-
gnanimes, reuerends Pre-
lats, nobles Seigneurs, Iu-
ſticiers honorables, vene-
rables Bourgeois, loyaux
Marchans, & ſimple po-
pulaire: ceſt a vous hommes, c'eſt a vous fem-
mes, c'eſt a vous filles, & enfans, de quelque
aage que ce ſoit, c'eſt a tous en general & chacun a part ſoy, que pour le bien public ie voüe
& conſacre ce mien eſcript couché en peu de
termes: lequel ie vous ſupplie vouloir accepter
d'auſſi bon cueur que ie le vous preſente : &
comme œuure mis en auant , non point pour

The 1558 booklet calling the prophet Monstradamus

Chapter 18.

Pseudo-Methodius

*T*he prophecy attributed to Bemechobus, usually called Bishop Methodius of Patara, who died in the 4th century, is the Pseudo-Methodius prophecy. According to the book *Fin du monde et signes des temps - visionnaires et prophètes en France méridionale (fin XIIIe - début XV siècle) Cahiers de Fanjeaux - vol 27*, published in 1992, this is a Syriac text, and it was translated in the 7th century under the name of Doctrine. Bernard McGinn calls this treatise "the crown of Eastern Christian apocalyptic literature." This prophecy seems to be one of the earliest surviving mentions to a Future World Emperor.

The text found below was translated by me directly from the *Liber Mirabilis,* but this version is different from other versions, for example, the E. Sackur version:

"This new Muslim invasion will be a punishment without limit and mercy. The Lord will surrender all the nations in the hands of these, because of the transgressions committed against His laws. This is why God gave us to the barbarians' powers, because we forgot His divine precepts. Because the Christians surrendered to a large number of illicit actions and they were dirtied with the most infamous indecencies, this is why the Lord put them in the hands of the Saracens. (...) Spain will be destroyed. France, Germany and Gothia, devoured by a thousand scourges, will see many of their inhabitants leaving their lands. Romans will be killed or will flee. They will pursue their enemies until the sea islands, the Muslims will invade, at the same time, the north and the East, the south and the West. Jerusalem will

transport the prisoners of all nations that will be under its yoke and its tributaries. All of the treasures and all of the ornaments of the churches, in gold, silver, in precious stones, will become their property; the desolation will be large, churches set on fire, and the followers' divestment thrown there where nobody will be found for burying them. (...) This way, the whole land will be given to the Muslims, who will seize it, which will destroy it. This is why the Lord called Ishmael, his father, Instrument of war; and many cities will be destroyed, therefore the children of the desert will come, and these are not men, but hateful beings to men. They will kill even pregnant women and they will immolate the priests in the shrine. They will profane the churches and will violate women, and they will wear, they and their wives, sacred ornaments. (...) This will be, among the Christians who inhabit on the earth, a general tribulation. It is then that it will be perfectly distinguished who really believes on the Lord. Because the Lord won't send these tribulations to the Christians to kill the believers; but to be sure about who are the most faithful believers: because the truth says her same: you will be blessed when you are pursued because of my name; and in fact the prophets who preceded us were pursued, or the one who perseveres until the end will be saved. But after these days of tribulation, when the Muslims, dresses in bright garments of purple and gold, and as engaged couples, glorify themselves of their victories everywhere, referring to the Christians who could not be protected against their powers, they will say: "quickly in our power we conquered the land and all who inhabit on it"; then Lord will remember, in His mercy, of His promise to those who adore him, to those that have faith in Christ and He will free them of the yoke of the Saracens.

In France, a people of Christians will appear who will fight them, will kill them, will free their arrested wives and will massacre their children. At the same time, the Muslims will be killed and they will know the tribulation. And the Lord will return to them the evil that they will have done, in a proportion seven times larger. The Lord will give them to the powers of the Christians, whose empire will be elevated above all of the empires. The yoke that the Christians will impose will be them hard and those who remain will be slave. The land, before destroyed by them, will be pacified then. The enemies' *prisoners will return to their homeland, and the population will grow and multiply.*

The Roman King (Great Monarch) will show a great indignation against those who will have denied Christ in Egypt or in Arabia. The peace and the peacefulness will be reborn on the earth, as there was never before, as there will never be: happiness and joy will be everywhere. The world will be free of tribulations."

Chapter 19.

Signa Judicii

---

*D*uring the Middle Ages, prophecies announcing the signs that would be preceding the end of the world circulated handwritten in Latin and in other languages in Europe. One of the most famous of these manuscripts was the *Signa Iudicii or Judicii* (Signs of the Judgment). Although the oldest surviving version of this manuscript is from the 11th century, according to some writers, *Signa Judicii* was based on a lost book written by Saint Jerome (347-420), the translator of the first Bible into Latin, known as *Vulgata,* the Catholic Church official version of the Bible until 1995. William W. Heist found 120 different versions of the *Signa Judicii* that can be classified in eight families.[39]

The manuscript is a list of 15 signs that would occur before or after the coming of the Antichrist, and they consisted basically of a huge flood and an earthquake that would shake the whole planet.

Concerning this prophecy, Gonzalo de Berceo played an important role. Gonzalo, born in Berceo, in Spain, was a friar and one of the most cultured poets of the 13th century. Several works

---

[39] This number shows that this was a manuscript commonly copied and well-known in the Middle Ages. In fact, it influenced the Legenda Aurea section of prophecies.

are attributed to him, among them *Signos que aparecerán antes del Juicio Final (Signs which will appear before the Final Judgment).* According to Gonzalo, he became aware of this prophecy *"reading a precious booklet written by Saint Jerome, which established the signs of the judgment..."*[40]

The first sign says that the sea will grow reaching the clouds, surpassing the mountains and anyone who sees this happening will be frightened. Then, the sea will go down, as much as it was raised up. The third sign says that the fish will swim to the surface of the sea. Soon afterwards, there will be such abnormal behavior of birds and animals, that will make a great noise. Then, seas and rivers will increase their power. The fifth sign refers to the trees and green vegetables, which will acquire a bloody color. Soon afterwards, it will be a day of darkness. And everything will be destroyed to its foundation. The stones will be changed into powder in the seventh sign. On the eighth sign, there will be a very strong shaking all over the world. In the ninth sign, hills will become plains. Soon afterwards, the people will be mute. On the eleventh sign, the sepulchers will be open and bones will be seen. The twelfth sign speaks of stars that will be moved or will fall from the sky. Then, people, vegetables and animals will die. In the last sign, the angel will blow his apocalyptic trumpet.

Another sign mentioned in Signa Judicii is the darkening of the sun. Maybe the "end" has already happened other times in the past, and for this reason, in the whole planet, the darkening of the sun means the same threat: this is what many peoples called past "ends of the world". The sun disappears for three or four days in

---

[40] Although I couldn't verify the authenticity of this prophecy and a few authors doubt it was really written by Jerome, the well-known French Historian Jacques Le Goff states in his book about Medieval Civilization that Saint Jerome really wrote about this in the Annales of the Hebrew People. Other writers have said the same.

many myths of a past catastrophe, until it shines again. In Antilles, the reason of the temporary death of the sun is the demon Majoba. For the South American Indians Tupis, it is an "ounce", a large feline. In Cambodia, it is the star Rahu. In Borneo, a winged serpent. In Indonesia, a serpent with paws. In Egypt, it is the dragon Apophis and in China it is the toad Tchen-tchou. In Himalaya, the reason for the temporary lack of sunlight is the giant Tamu-sobato and in Tunisia it is a witch. When the Spaniards arrived in America, they were impressed with the fear that the natives had of eclipses. Inca, for example, means Son of the Sun and they prayed for the sun to keep shining and not die.

Chapter 20.

Saint Francis Xavier

---

*B*orn in the Basque country, Spain, Francis Xavier (1506-1552) was sent by the king of Portugal to Portuguese India. It seems that the missionary wrote this prophecy there, at least supposing that the Latin manuscript that I found in a European library is authentic. There are variations of this prophecy in the manuscripts that contain it, they do not match exactly in contents although they are very similar. This prophecy is very rare and ignored by writers and it is certainly one of the oldest prophecies with the word "America", maybe the oldest one, if authentic. It is probably also the oldest prophecy ever mentioning that the Muslim powers will arrive in America.

I never saw this prophecy published in any book of prophecies and this is probably the first time it is published in English, translated here by me from Latin.

"The kingdom given by God will bloom until the end. Suddenly, it will be destroyed by Muslims. A destructive lion will come[41] and it will nail their claws in the enemies... Easy and horribly, the (European) land will be occupied and destroyed... The kingdom will be oppressed and there will be confusion. The Prince will make the enemies return to their lands... the empire will shake and it will suffer with the catastrophic invasion from the East that will reach America, and will reach their objective... There will

---

[41] the Great Monarch, i.e., the messianic King.

appear great signs in the sky. In two years of misery, the empire of the iniquitous ones will be infested all around the sides... Rome will be destroyed."

The manuscript in Latin

Chapter 21.

Marie-Julie J. de la Fraudais

*B*orn in France in 1850 and died in 1941, this religious woman had many prophetic visions in ecstasy, usually related to France, but not only. The prophecies she said were well documented books written by Pierre Roberdel and published in France.[42] She was a very simple religious woman.

Concerning what could be the third world war, Christ told her:

"The punishments will begin in Paris. Punishments in the southern cities. What a slaughter! In France there will be more bloodshed than in Rome. But this won't last much. The foreigner will enter in France with his whole army. There will be a gap measured by me. I will stop them and then, I will make the Savior (King) to be born among my children. He will cross the east and will seem to come from the north. I will drive him to the south of France and, from there, I will revitalize him... not on today's throne, because there won't be a throne anymore, not even a base to establish another one. It will be in this third crisis (war) that the salvation will come. He will come from my Sacred Heart... that is destined to bring the peace. Once he is crowned, the evils will finish. He descends from Saint Louis[43] but he doesn't know this guilty Sodome".

---

[42] ROBERDEL, Pierre. *Les prophéties de la Fraudais.* Montsurs: Éditions Résiac, 1981

[43] French king killed during the French Revolution. According to some historians, he had a son who escaped the prison in the Temple helped by a woman. Some said he survived.

"The fire will fall from the sky on Sodome. (...) The fire from the sky will join the fire from the earth."

About the Great Monarch:

"God hides who He will choose to save the Church and to reign over France, to remove the demon's power from the whole world. (...) He will come from the race of Saint Louis. (...) The King will arrive with a small procession of lively men, like him, for God's sake and wanting only the glory of God. (...) But before this happening, three sovereigns (false or temporary kings) should appear, full of human ambitions and knowing only human means."

A message to the sister:

"I am the King of the Universe. I wanted to give to France a king that she refused; but she will accept the one I want to give, she will ask for him, she will put him in her heart. But before this king, there will be a crisis and a violent storm in France..."

Message of Jesus about what seems to be the third world war and about natural catastrophes:

"As soon as My people fell in the indifference, I began to threaten it; Today it deserves My Justice! I will have mercy of the good people, but I will devour the others; the land will open up and it will disappear forever! I will be moved, but only after the destruction and the punishment that I promised! I will destroy everything on the earth; it will be introduced in a grave, from where, after purified with blood, I will resuscitate her gloriously, as well as I did to Me! The desolation will be so big that many people will dry frightened and will believe that this is the end of the world!

The earth will be a vast cemetery. Corpses of Heretics and fair people will cover it. The land will shake and, then, great waves will agitate the sea and will invade the continents."

About the three days of darkness:

"There will be three days of continuous darkness: during three nights and two days there will be a continuous night. The sacred candles and only them will be able to light up during this horrible darkness. A candle will be enough for the three days, but in the heretics' houses, they won't burn. In these three days of darkness the demons will appear with the most hateful and amazing forms. You will hear through the airs the most horrible blasphemies. Neither the wind, nor the storm, nor the earthquakes can turn off the light from the sacred candles. Clouds red as blood will cross the Sky; the sound of the thunder will shake the earth; sinister rays will furrow the clouds. The earth will be turned over in their foundations; the sea will lift deafening waves that will invade the continent. The blood will run with so much abundance that it will reach men's waist. The land will become an immense cemetery. The corpses of the fair people and the heretics will cover the soil. The hunger that she will come will be big. Finally, everything will be changed and three forths of humankind will perish.

The crisis will break out almost suddenly; the punishments will be for everyone, happening in an uninterrupted way... there will be diabolical prodigies in the airs. Bodies will rise in the air. The friends of the Lord should not see these prodigies, which will be the announcement of the wrath of God and the punishments. More of the half of the French people will die, it will hardly survive one fourth. The great blow of the Hand of God won't take long, but, it will be so terrible that many will be rotten in fright!"

"Tus... Tusca... Tuscany.

I read it well, I don't know what this means, but I go on. Tuscany... the earth shakes, it is swallowed, it is lost in an unexplainable hole. The frightened people flee to the proximities of the Eternal City. In the city of Sienne – I don't know where it is – the earth will open as big graves full of a filthy smell d'une odeur infecte. (...) In Brittany, the shaking will be felt, but not far».

Chapter 22.

Leonardo da Vinci

*L*eonardo, born in 1452 in the small village called Vinci, near Florence, has always been seen as someone intelligent. Author of the most famous painting in the world, the Mona Lisa or Gioconda, his drawings about future machines reveal an incredible imagination, intelligence and maybe the ability of predicting the future. Some people consider him the most intelligent person of all times. The Da Vinci prophecies are found scattered in manuscript codex and they were published for the first time in Italy in 1899 in the book called *Frammenti letterari e filosofici*, written by Edmondo Solmi. The book prepared by Solmi was probably based on The Literary Works of Leonardo da Vinci (London, 1883), written by Jean Paul Richter, and on the publication as fac-simile of the leonardian codex, kept in France, in 1881.

I translated some of the prophecies from the Solmi book, but the 1925 edition reprinted years later. Some prophecies were left out because they don't seem to make sense:

Prophecies about strange animals (genetic engineering or tanks and planes?)

From the land animals dressed in darkness will come out, which in wonderful assaults, will attack the human generation, and through terrible bites and bloodshed, will devour them.

Through the air the flying specimens will go, which will attack men and animals, from which they will feed voraciously: full will be their intestines will red blood.

Many men will be seen in animals moving very quickly towards the end of their lives and in a very quick death. Through the air (planes) and over the land (tanks) animals will be seen in many colors carrying ferociously the men to the destruction of their lives.

Huge bodies without life will be seen carrying ferociously many men to the destruction of their lives.

Prophecies about what seem to be the consequence of chemical weapons used in a future war:

A terrible illness will come to mankind, so that they will lacerate themselves with their own nails.

Men will throw away their own food.

Many people will die with the head broken, and their eyes will be out of their head, because of frightening animals that will come from the darkness.
Many peoples will hide themselves with their families and food inside dark caves; and there, in the dark places, they will eat with their families during many months, without any other natural or artificial light.

Prophecies about the pole shift or a natural catastrophe concerning the sea waters:

The sea water will raise over the peak of the hills towards the sky and will fall over the people homes.

And many animals from the land and the sea will raise to the stars.

Darkness will come from the East with so much obscurity that it will cover the sky over Italy.

The land that is under will be over again, and concerning the opposite hemispheres...

The sky over a big part of Africa will change, and this sky will go towards Europe, and the European sky will go towards Africa, the sky from the provinces will mix themselves with a big revolution.

At the end, the land will be red due to the warming of many days, and the stones will turn into ashes.

The water animals will die in the boiling waters.

The mud will be so large that men will walk over trees in their lands.

There will be a strong wind, and through this the Eastern things will become Western....

All elements will be mixed together in a big revolution, going in one time towards the center of the world, another time towards the sky, and when the Southern parts will go fiercely against the Northern cold, the East will go to the West, and this hemisphere will go to the other hemisphere.

All men will change hemispheres immediately.

All of the animals will move from the East to the West, and those from the South will go to the North.

Prophecies about a future (or present) communication system in the world:

Men will move without walking, they will speak to people who are not present, they will listen to the one who is not speaking.

Men will talk one to another in very distant lands and they will answer.

Men will talk and touch and hug themselves, being far, each one in each hemisphere, and understand each other's language.

Chapter 23.

Alois Irlmaier

---

*A*lois Irlmaier (1894-1959) was a simple Christian man who lived in Freilassing, Germany. During his life, he helped the police to locate bandits, he helped diagnosing ill people and he predicted about the third world war, which according to him, would break out soon after the murder of a "big one anywhere near to the Arab lands".

Initially, Irlmaier said that the beginning of the third world war would be in 1950. He was wrong. After that, he preferred to not say anything about the time when it would break out, being very careful with years and dates. Later, he said that he was seeing an 8 and two 9s. This could mean August of 99 and could be related to Vladimir Putin, because Putin became the Primie Minister of Russia in August 1999. A prophecy saying that he was seeing three 9s (and not one 8 and two 9s) was also attributed to him, but in a German book considered a good and serious one, it says that he probably said 899.

Irlmaier was famous in his time in Germany. Newspapers published articles about the seer who could answer questions posed by others, as we can see here at the end of this chapter some pages.

"Suddenly, a new war in the Middle East begins, large naval forces are positioned in a hostile way in the Mediterranean Sea - the situation is tense. (...) The third murder happens. Then, the war breaks out. (...) Immediately, the revenge arrives along the great waters. Meanwhile, the yellow dragon

invades Alaska and Canada at the same time. (...) white pigeons fly (...) and soon afterwards it rains a yellow powder on a line. When the city of gold (Prague or New York) is destroyed, it begins. As a yellow line, it reaches the city in the bay. (...) When it falls, everything dies, trees, bushes, flocks, any vegetation, everything turns dry and black. The houses still exist. I don't know what is this, therefore I don't know how to say. It is a long line. What is on this line, dies. (...) The airplanes drop a yellow powder between the Black Sea and the Northern Sea. Soon afterwards, a mortal strip is created, from the Black Sea to the Northern Sea, as wide as half of Bavaria. In this area, vegetation cannot grow anymore, the humans will live alone. The Russian attack is continuous. (...) Here, the pilots also throw their black boxes. They don't explode, but before touching the soil, they spread a smoke or dust yellow greenish. For one year, no organism can enter in this area, otherwise it will be exposed to the high mortal danger. (...) These boxes are satanic. When they explode, a greenish-yellow powder or smoke spreads, and everything that gets in contact with this thing dies, human beings, animals and vegetables. The humans get very black and the meat falls from their bones, so strong is the poison.

An airplane, coming from the East, throw something in the sea. Then, the waters rise so high as a tower and fall. Everything is flooded. There is a earthquake. The south of England is swallowed by the waters. Three great cities are ruined: one will destroyed by the waters and the second is located in a point so that you will see only the Church tower and the third one sinking.

Part of England disappears, when the thing, which the pilot drops, falls in the sea. Then the waters raise, growing so much as a tower and they fall. What is this thing, I don't know... The coastal cities are strongly menaced by waters, the sea is very agitated, the waves are so high as a house; It bubbles as it was boiling in the depths. Islands disappear and the weather change. Part of the proud island sinks when this thing falls in the sea, which the pilot drops.

"The city with the iron tower (Paris) becomes the victim of its own people. They set fire on everything. The revolution is violent. The islands coasts are invaded by the waters, because the waters will be very violent. I see large holes

in the sea, that close when the enormous waves return. The beautiful city in the blue sea sinks almost completely in the sea, in dirt and in sand, that are ejected by the sea. I see three cities sinking in the south, in the north and in the west. The big city with the high tower of iron is set on fire. But their own people did that, not those who came from the East. And the city is devastated, this I see well clearly."

"(...) In Italy, the situation is agitated too. They kill many people and Pope flees, but many religious people will be killed, many churches are destroyed".

"After the victory, an emperor is crowned by Pope who fled. The laws that bring death to the children are extinguished after the cleaning. There will be peace. A good time. The Pope, who had to flee through the waters for a long period, come back. When the flowers bloom in the prairies, he will return and will lament his murdered brothers.

On the conversion in Russia after the war:
"In Russia, they begin a revolution and a civil war. The bodies are so many that it is not possible to remove them from the highways. The cross comes to honor again. The Russians believe in God again. The largest, among the leaders of the party, commit suicide and in blood, the great criminals are washed. I see a red mass, mixed with yellow faces, it is a general conflict and a horrible slaughter. Then, they sing the song of Easter and they burn candles in front of sacred images. Through the prayer of Christianity, the beast of hell dies; besides, the youths believe again in the mother's of God intercession".

On the three days of darkness:
"There will be darkness one day, during the war. Then hail will fall with rays and thunders and an earthquake will shake the Earth. Then don't leave house! There won't be light anymore, except from candles, the electric current will be cut. The one who breathes the dust strongly, will suffer cramps and will die. Don't open the window, cover it with black paper. All the water exposed will be poisoned as well as every food not canned. Also the food in glass or in glasses; they will be affected because the glass won't protect. Outside there will be death for the powder; many people will die. After 72

hours, everything will be finished. But, I say once again: don't leave your home, don't look outside through the window, let the consecrated candles or the wax candle burn. And pray. In that night more people will die than in the two world wars.

The water from the piping system is drinkable, but not the milk. Truly, people won't be very hungry during the catastrophe and the darkness. During 72 hours don't open the window. (...) The cattle falls around, the grass becomes yellow and dry, the corpses completely yellow and black. The wind blows the clouds of death to the East."

Er spürt das Wasser und er sieht die Zukunft...

Der berühmteste Mann Freilassings - Brunnenbauer, Wassersucher und Heilseher

Der Brunnenbauer Alois Irlmeier erzählt: „... das eine sag i dir ganz genau: Bei uns da werd so guad koin ans net gschegn ..."

Page of a newspaper (1949) with the title *He pours down the water and sees the future* and a photo of the prophet.

Der Nostradamus von Freilassing

Besuch beim Brunnenmacher Alois Irlmaier · Von Herbert Frank

Here, in the *Bayerische Heimat* published in October 1949, Alois Irlmaier is called "The Nostradamus of Freilassing", the place where he lived.

Irlmaier prophezeit über den nächsten Welt-krieg und seine politischen Auswirkungen

Unsere nachfolgenden Aufzeichnungen einiger Prophezeiungen Irlmaiers über einen eventuell anbrechenden dritten Weltkrieg sollen vor allem den Chronisten einer späteren Zeit dienen. Ihnen allein ist es vorbehalten, über die politischen Gesichte des Freilassinger Hellsehers ein gerechtes Urteil zu bilden. Wir können sie nur ermitteln und auf den Prüfstand der Zukunft legen. Auch bei Berücksichtigung der im letzten Kapitel erwähnten Fälle, die fast durchwegs für eine hohe hellseherische Veranlagung Irlmaiers sprechen, wäre es verantwortungslos, wollte man ihn als Prophet unseres Schicksals propagieren. Die Geschichte liegt in der Hand unberechenbarer Mächte. Ein Hellseher kann im besten Falle nur Bruchteile ihrer künftigen Entwicklung schauen, und ist auch dabei abhängig von seiner persönlichen Vorstellungswelt, vom Milieu seiner Umgebung und — von der Macht des Irrtums. Allein der Umstand, daß bei Irlmaiers politischen Voraussagen der in bäuerlichen Kreisen Südbayerns immer noch aufrecht erhaltene Wunschtraum einer Monarchie mit klerikalen Einflüssen spukt, reizt zur Annahme, daß dieser Hellseher zu stark von persönlichen Hoffnungen abhängig ist, als daß er seine Gesichte frei entfalten lassen könnte.

Auf unsere Frage, ob er denn an einen dritten Weltkrieg glaube, sagte Irlmaier: „Die Leut' meinen immer, daß alles so werden müßte, wie sie es wünschen. Ich aber seh' genau, daß ein neuer Krieg über uns kommen wird. Zuerst bringen's noch den Dritten um, auch einen Hochgestellten. Zwei hams schon ermordet. Da drüben muß er d'ran glauben, wo die Sonne aufgeht, und dann bricht's los über Nacht. Grausam wird der Krieg werden."

Hier muß erwähnt werden, daß Irlmaier bei der Schilderung seiner politischen Gesichte einem fast näselnden Ton verfällt, etwas leiser spricht und manchmal sogar versucht, sich in Reimen auszudrücken. Wir wollen zu Gunsten einer besseren Verständlichkeit auf einen Teil der persönlichen Note seines Vortrages verzichten.

„Drei große Heereszüge seh' ich in weiten Zangen bis zum Ruhrgebiet vorstoßen. Über dem großen Wasser da drüben, da kommt der Ruß' noch hin. Von der Tschechei hinauf nach Norden wird's menschenleer werden, dort wird's grün und gelb niedergeh'n, sogar das Gras seh' ich dort absterben. Kein Wurm, kein Strauch, kein Baum wird bleiben, alles werden sie vernichten, die großen weißen Tauben. Von den drei Heereszügen wird keiner mehr die Heimat seh'n. Wir aber haben nichts zu befürchten, denn das Land zwischen Untersberg und Wendelstein wird beschützt bleiben vom heiligen Gnadenbild in Altötting."

21

Chapter 24.

George Washington

*F*irst Pesident of the United States, he was born in 1732 and died in 1799. The following prophecy is said to be originally published by Wesley Bradshaw in June 1861 in the Philadelphia Inquirer.

First Pesident of the United States, Washington was born in 1732 and died in 1799. According to the tradition, the account of this prophecy was given to Bradshaw by an old soldier, Anthony Sherman. Some scholars believe this was a work of fiction created by Charles W. Alexander44 (1836-1927), a Philadelphia journalist writing under the pseudonym of Wesley Bradshaw. Also, there seems to lack an eighteenth-century evidence that corroborates this story.

"From the opening of the Revolution we experienced all phases of fortune, now good and now ill; one time victorious and another conquered. The darkest period we had, I think, was when Washington, after several reverses, retreated to Valley Forge, where he resolved to spend the winter of 1777. Ah! I have often seen our dear commander's care-worn cheeks, as he would be conversing with a confidential officer about the condition of his poor soldiers. You have doubtless heard the story of Washington's going to the thicket to pray. Well, it was not only true, but he used often to pray in secret for aid and comfort from God, the interposition of whose Divine Providence brought us

---

[44] A biographer says Charles W. Alexander, journalist in Philadelphia, was involved in Philadelphia journalism from 1821 to the 1850s. Others say he was born in 1836. So maybe these two journalists are not the same person.

safely through the darkest days of tribulation. "One day, I remember well, the chilly winds whistled through the leafless trees, though the sky was cloudless and the sun shone brightly, he remained in his quarters nearly all the afternoon alone. When he came out, I noticed that his face was a shade paler than usual, and there seemed to be something on his mind of more than ordinary importance. Returning just after dusk, he dispatched an orderly to the quarters of the officer I mention who was presently in attendance. After a preliminary conversation of about half an hour, Washington, gazing upon his companion with that strange look of dignity which he alone could command said to the latter: "'I do not know whether it is owing to anxiety of my mind, or what, but this afternoon, as I was sitting at this table engaged in preparing a dispatch, something seemed to disturb me. Looking up, I beheld standing opposite me a singularly beautiful female. So astonished was I, for I had given strict orders not to be disturbed, that it was some moments before I found language to inquire the cause of her presence. A second, a third, and even a fourth time did I repeat my question, but received no answer from my mysterious visitor except a slight raising of her eyes. "'Presently I heard a voice saying, "Son of the Republic, look and learn," while at the same time my visitor extended her arm eastwardly. I now beheld a heavy white vapor at some distance rising fold upon fold. This gradually dissipated, and I looked upon a strange scene. Before me lay spread out in one vast plain all the countries of the world---Europe, Asia, Africa, and America. I saw rolling and tossing, between Europe and America, the billows of the Atlantic, and between Asia and America lay the Pacific. ""Son of the Republic," said the same mysterious voice as before, "look and learn." At that moment I beheld a dark, shadowy being, like an angel, standing, or rather floating, in the hollow air, between Europe and America. Dipping water out of the ocean in the hollow of each hand, he sprinkled some upon America with his right hand while with his left hand he cast some on Europe. Immediately a cloud raised from these countries and joined in mid-ocean. For a while it remained stationary, and then moved slowly westward, until it enveloped America in its murky folds. Sharp flashes of lightning gleamed through it at intervals, and I heard the smothered groans and cries of the American people. "'A second time the angel dipped water from the ocean, and sprinkled it out as before. The dark cloud was then drawn back to the ocean, in whose heaving billows it sank from view. A third time I heard the mysterious voice saying, "Son of the Republic, look and learn." I cast my eyes upon America and beheld villages and towns and cities springing up one after another until the whole land, from the Atlantic to the Pacific, was dotted with them. Again I head the mysterious voice say, "Son of the Republic, the end of the century cometh, look and learn." "'At this the dark shadowy angel turned his face southward, and from Africa I saw an ill-omened specter approach our land. It flitted slowly over every town and city of the latter. The inhabitants presently set themselves in battle array against each other. As I continued looking, I saw a bright angel, on whose brow rested a crown of light, on which was traced the word "Union," bearing the American flag which he placed between the divided nation, and said, "Remember ye are brethren." Instantly, the inhabitants casting from them their weapons became friends once more, and united around the National Standard. "'And again I heard the mysterious voice saying, "Son of the Republic, look and learn." At this, the dark, shadowy angel placed a trumpet to his mouth and blew three distinct blasts; and taking water from the ocean, he sprinkled it upon Europe, Asia, and Africa. Then my eyes beheld a fearful scene. From each of these countries arose thick, black clouds that were soon joined into one. And throughout this mass, there gleamed a dark red light by which I saw hordes of armed men, who, moving with the cloud, marched by land and sailed by sea to America, which country was enveloped in the volume of cloud. And I dimly saw these vast armies devastate the whole country, and burn the villages, towns and cities that I beheld springing up. "'As my ears listened to the thundering of the cannon, clashing of swords, and the shouts and cries of millions in mortal combat., I again heard the mysterious voice saying, "Son of the Republic, look and learn." When the voice had ceased, the dark shadowy angel placed his trumpet once more to his mouth, and blew a long and fearful blast. "'Instantly a light as of a thousand suns shone down from above me, and pierced and broke into fragments the dark cloud which enveloped America. At the same moment the angel upon whose head still shone the word "Union," and who bore our national flag in one hand and a sword in the other, descended from the heavens attended by legions of white spirits. These immediately joined the inhabitants of America, who I perceived were well-nigh overcome, but who immediately taking courage again closed up their broken ranks and renewed the battle. Again, amid the fearful noise of the conflict, I heard the mysterious voice saying, "Son of the Republic, look and learn." "'As the voice ceased, the shadowy angel for the last time dipped water from the ocean and sprinkled it upon America. Instantly the dark cloud rolled back, together with the armies it had brought, leaving the inhabitants of the land victorious. "'Then once more I beheld the villages, towns and cities, springing up where I had seen them before, while the bright angel, plating the azure standard he had brought in the midst of them, cried with a loud voice: "While the stars remain, and the heavens send down dew upon the earth, so long shall the Union last." And taking from his brow the crown on which was blazoned the word "Union," he placed it upon the Standard, while the people, kneeling down, said "Amen." "'The scene instantly began to fade and dissolve, and I at last saw nothing but the rising, curling vapor I at first beheld. This also disappearing, I found myself once more gazing upon the mysterious visitor, who in the same voice I had heard before, said, "Son of the Republic, what you have seen is thus interpreted. Three great perils will come upon the Republic. The most fearful is the third." "(The comment on his word 'third' is: The help against the THIRD peril comes in the shape of Divine assistance; passing which, the whole world united shall not prevail against her. Let every child of the Republic learn to live for his God, his land and Union.)" "'With these words the vision vanished, and I started from my seat and felt that I had seen a vision wherein had been shown me the birth, progress, and destiny of the UNITED STATES." "Such, my friends," concluded the venerable narrator, "were the words I heard from Washington's own lips, and America will do well to profit by them."

Chapter 25.

Legenda Aurea

*T*his is not a book on prophecies, but about lives of saints. It was a medieval best-seller in the manuscript form and among the first printed books, in the years 1470-1500 it was the most printed book in Europe, with more than 150 editions, even more than the Bible. It was written in the 13th century and since then to the invention of the press machines, it was a widely copied manuscript, which attests how important it was from 1300 to 1500.

Although the Legenda Aurea, also known as Golden Legend in English, was not a book of prophecies, in the beginning of it there is a section containing prophecies about the Antichrist and the signs of the end of the world, two of the most frequent apocalyptical Medieval themes.

The book was originally written in Latin by a priest and archbishop called Jacob Voragine (or Varagine, born in 1230 in Varaggio, Italy and died in 1298). Here is part of the prophecies.

"As for the first, three things shall happen before the Judgment. First, the terrible confusion of signs and tokens. Secondly, the malice and deceit of Antichrist, and the third, of vehement and marvelous operation of the fire. As touching the signs, S. Luke saith in the twenty-fifth chapter: Erunt signa in sole, luna et stellis, etc. There shall be great signs in the sun, in the moon, and in the stars, and in the earth oppression of people worried for the confusion of the sound of the sea and of the waves. The three first signs be determined in the Book of the Apocalypse in the sixth chapter. Sol factus est niger tanquam

saccus cilicinus: et luna facta est sicut sanguis, et stellæ ceciderunt super terraim. Then shall be the time that the sun shall be black as a sack, gross and rude, and the moon shall be as blood, and the stars shall fall on the earth. The sun is said dark, forasmuch as he is deprived of his light, as though he wept for the dying of men. For S. Austin saith that, the vengeance of God shall be so cruel at the day of doom, that the sun shall not dare behold it. Or as for to speak of the proper signification spiritually to be understood, is that, the Son of Justice, Jesu Christ, shall be then so dark that no man shall dare know him. The heaven is here taken for the air, and the star judge in great fear. The sixth sign, the edifices and buildings shall fall down: and in this sixth day thunders and tempests full of fire shall grow in the west, where the sun goeth down against the firmament, in running to the east. The seventh sign, the stones shall smite and hurtle together and shall cleave in four parts, and each part shall smite other. The eighth sign shall be the moving and general trembling of the earth, which shall be so. The ninth sign, all the earth shall be even and plain, and all the mountains and valleys shall be brought into powder and be all like. The tenth day, the men shall issue out of the caves and shall go by the ways and fields as men aliened and out of their wit, and shall not con speak one to another. The eleventh day the bones of dead men shall issue out of their burials and places and shall hold them upon their sepulchers, and from the sun rising unto it go down, the sepulchers shall be open, to the end that the dead bodies may all issue. The twelfth sign all the stars shall fall from the heaven and shall spread out rays of fire, and then great quantity shall grow. In this twelfth day it is said that all the beasts shall come to the field howling, and shall not eat ne drink. The thirteenth sign, all living shall die, to the end that they should arise with the dead bodies. The fourteenth day the heaven and the earth shall burn. The fifteenth day shall be a new heaven and a new earth, and all things and all dead men shall arise.

(...) Antichrist; he shall pain him to deceive all men by four manners. The first manner shall be by suasion and false exposition of Scripture. Forasmuch as he may, he shall give them to understand Christ, and he shall destroy the law of Jesu Christ, and shall ordain his law in alleging David the Prophet that saith: *Constitue domine legislatorem super eos.* Thus shall he say, that it was said for him as he that was ordained of God for to set law upon his place, after this that is said in the scripture of Daniel, Daniel xi.: *Dabunt abominationem et desolationem templi, etc.* Antichrist and his complices shall give abomination and desolation to the temple of God in this time, as saith the gloss: Antichrist shall be in the temple of God, as God, for that he shall destroy the law of God. The second manner shall be by marvelous operation of miracles, whereof saith the apostle S. Paul in his second Epistle *ad Thessalonicenses* in the second chapter, where he saith: *Cujus adventus erit secundum operationem Sathanae in omnibus verbis et prodigiis mendacibus.* Of Antichrist it is said that, the coming shall be after the operation of Satan in all his signs, in all his marvels, and false Iying deeds, whereof S. John maketh mention in the Apocalypse, the thirteenth chapter: *Fecit signa ut etiam ignem facerit de celo in terram descendere.* Antichrist shall make such signs, that is to say, he shall make such tokens that he shall make the fire descend from heaven. The gloss saith that, like as the Holy Ghost descended in likeness of fire, in likewise shall Antichrist give the evil spirit in likeness of fire. The third manner that he shall do for to deceive, shall be in giving of gifts, of which is written in the book of Daniel the Prophet in his eleventh chapter: *Dabit eis potestatem in multis et terram divides gratuito:* Antichrist shall give puissance to his servants in many things, and shall depart the earth to them after his will. The gloss saith that, Antichrist shall give many gifts to them that he shall deceive. And to his disciples he shall divide the earth, and them that and make them thereby to obey him. The fourth manner for to deceive them shall be by torments that he shall give to them, whereof Daniel saith in his eighth chapter: *Supra quod credi potest universe vastabit;* no man shall believe how he shall destroy and torment them that will not believe in him, for to draw them to him by force. And S. Gregory saith of him: *Robustos quippe interficiet, et cetera;* he shall slay the great and strong men; when he may not win nor overcome them by heart ne will, he shall overcome them by torment. The third thing that shall go before the judgment shall be the right vehement fire, the which shall go tofore the face of the judge. And God shall send this fire for four causes. First for the renewing of the world, for he shall purge and renew the elements. And, like to the form of the deluge it shall be forty cubits higher than all the mountains, like as it is written in the history scholastic; for the works of the people may mount so high. Secondly for the purgation of the people; for then that fire shall be instead of the fire of purgatory to them that then shall be on live. Thirdly for to give more greater torment to them that be damned. Fourthly for to give more clearness and light unto the saints."

14th century Manuscript – Legenda Aurea – Annunciation

Prophétie de Béranger.

Faites l'aumône au dernier de vos roi.
BÉRANGER

Prophecy found in a book printed in the 19th century

www.ingramcontent.com/pod-product-compliance
Lightning Source LLC
Chambersburg PA
CBHW072026040426
42447CB00009B/1754